Y0-BQW-885

THE AGE OF ANXIETY

A Baroque Eclogue

THE

AGE OF ANXIETY

A BAROQUE ECLOGUE

W. H. AUDEN

Lacrimosa dies illa
Qua resurget ex favilla
Iudicandus homo reus
Thomas a Celano (?)
Dies Irae

RANDOM HOUSE · NEW YORK

TENTH PRINTING

Acknowledgments are due to the *New Yorker* magazine and *Commonweal,* in which two extracts originally appeared under the titles *Spinster's Song* and *Metropolis,* respectively.

 PUBLISHED IN NEW YORK BY RANDOM HOUSE, INC., AND SIMULTANEOUSLY IN TORONTO, CANADA, BY RANDOM HOUSE OF CANADA, LIMITED, 1947.

MANUFACTURED IN THE UNITED STATES OF AMERICA BY KINGSPORT PRESS, INC., KINGSPORT, TENN.

A. B.

To

JOHN BETJEMAN

PART ONE

PROLOGUE

Now the day is over,
Night is drawing nigh,
Shadows of the evening
Steal across the sky.
S. Baring-Gould

WHEN THE HISTORICAL PROCESS breaks down and armies organize with their embossed debates the ensuing void which they can never consecrate, when necessity is associated with horror and freedom with boredom, then it looks good to the bar business.

In times of peace there are always a number of persons who wake up each morning excited by the prospect of another day of interesting and difficult work, or happily certain that the one with whom they shared their bed last night will be sharing it with them again the next, and who, in consequence, must be written off by the proprietor as a lost market. Not that he need worry. There will always be enough lonelies and enough failures who need desperately what he has to offer—namely, an unprejudiced space in which nothing particular ever happens, and a choice of physiological aids to the imagination whereby each may appropriate it for his or her private world of repentant felicitous forms, heavy expensive objects or avenging flames and floods—to guarantee him a handsome profit still.

But in war-time, when everybody is reduced to the anxious

status of a shady character or a displaced person, when even the most prudent become worshippers of chance, and when, in comparison to the universal disorder of the world outside, his Bohemia seems as cosy and respectable as a suburban villa, he can count on making his fortune.

Looking up from his drink, QUANT caught the familiar eye of his reflection in the mirror behind the bar and wondered why he was still so interested in that tired old widower who would never be more now than a clerk in a shipping office near the Battery.

More, that is, as a public figure: for as so often happens in the modern world—and how much restlessness, envy and self-contempt it causes—there was no one-to-one correspondence between his social or economic position and his private mental life. He had come to America at the age of six when his father, implicated somehow in the shooting of a landlord, had had to leave Ireland in a hurry, and, from time to time, images, some highly-colored, some violent, derived from a life he could not remember, would enter unexpectedly and incomprehensibly into his dreams. Then, again, in early manhood, when unemployed during a depression, he had spent many hours one winter in the Public Library reading for the most part—he could not have told you why—books on Mythology. The knowledge gained at that time had ever since lain oddly around in a corner of his mind like luggage left long ago in an emergency by some acquaintance and never reclaimed.

Watching the bubbles rise in his glass, MALIN was glad to

forget for his few days of leave the uniform of the Canadian Air Force he was wearing and the life it represented, at once disjointed and mechanical, alternately exhausting and idle, of a Medical Intelligence officer; trying to recapture the old atmosphere of laboratory and lecture hall, he returned with pleasure to his real interests.

Lighting a cigarette, ROSETTA, too, ignored her surroundings but with less ease. Yes, she made lots of money—she was a buyer for a big department store and did it very well—and that was a great deal, for, like anyone who has ever been so, she had a sensible horror of being poor. Yes, America was the best place on earth to come to if you had to earn your living, but did it have to be so big and empty and noisy and messy? Why could she not have been rich? Yes, though she was not as young as she looked, there were plenty of men who either were deceived or preferred a girl who might be experienced—which indeed she was. But why were the men one liked not the sort who proposed marriage and the men who proposed marriage not the sort one liked? So she returned now to her favorite day-dream in which she indulged whenever she got a little high—which was rather too often—and conjured up, detail by detail, one of those landscapes familiar to all readers of English detective stories, those lovely innocent countrysides inhabited by charming eccentrics with independent means and amusing hobbies to whom, until the sudden intrusion of a horrid corpse onto the tennis court or into the greenhouse, work and law and guilt are just literary words.

EMBLE, on the other hand, put down his empty glass and looked about him as if he hoped to read in all those faces the answer to his own disquiet. Having enlisted in the Navy during his sophomore year at a Mid-Western university, he suffered from that anxiety about himself and his future which haunts, like a bad smell, the minds of most young men, though most of them are under the illusion that their lack of confidence is a unique and shameful fear which, if confessed, would make them an object of derision to their normal contemporaries. Accordingly, they watch others with a covert but passionate curiosity. What makes them tick? What would it feel like to be a success? Here is someone who is nobody in particular, there even an obvious failure, yet they do not seem to mind. How is that possible? What is their secret?

In certain cases—his was one—this general unease of youth is only aggravated by what would appear to alleviate it, a grace of person which grants them, without effort on their part, a succession of sexual triumphs. For then the longing for success, the doubt of ever being able to achieve the kinds of success which have to be earned, and the certainty of being able to have at this moment a kind which does not, play dangerously into each other's hands.

So, fully conscious of the attraction of his uniform to both sexes, he looked round him, slightly contemptuous when he caught an admiring glance, and slightly piqued when he did not.

It was the night of All Souls.

QUANT was thinking:

My deuce, my double, my dear image,
Is it lively there, that land of glass
Where song is a grimace, sound logic
A suite of gestures? You seem amused.
How well and witty when you wake up,
How glad and good when you go to bed,
Do you feel, my friend? What flavor has
That liquor you lift with your left hand;
Is it cold by contrast, cool as this
For a soiled soul; does your self like mine
Taste of untruth? Tell me, what are you
Hiding in your heart, some angel face,
Some shadowy she who shares in my absence,
Enjoys my jokes? I'm jealous, surely,
Nicer myself (though not as honest),
The marked man of romantic thrillers
Whose brow bears the brand of a winter
No priest can explain, the poet disguised,
Thinking over things in thieves' kitchens,
Wanted by the waste, whom women's love
Or his own silhouette might all too soon
Betray to its tortures. I'll track you down,
I'll make you confess how much you know who
View my vices with a valet's slight
But shameless shrug, the *Schadenfreude*
Of cooks at keyholes. Old comrade, tell me
The lie of my lifetime but look me up in

Your good graces; agree to be friends
Till our deaths differ; drink, strange future,
To your neighbor now.

MALIN was thinking: No chimpanzee
Thinks it thinks. Things are divisible,
Creatures are not. In chaos all bodies
Would differ in weight. Dogs can learn to
Fear the future. The faceless machine
Lacks a surround. The laws of science have
Never explained why novelty always
Arrives to enrich (though the wrong question
Initiates nothing). Nature rewards
Perilous leaps. The prudent atom
Simply insists upon its safety now,
Security at all costs; the calm plant
Masters matter then submits to itself,
Busy but not brave; the beast assures
A stabler status to stolen flesh,
Assists though it enslaves: singular then
Is the human way; for the ego is a dream
Till a neighbor's need by name create it;
Man has no mean; his mirrors distort;
His greenest arcadias have ghosts too;
His utopias tempt to eternal youth
Or self-slaughter.

ROSETTA was thinking: From Seager's Folly

We beheld what was ours. Undulant land
Rose layer by layer till at last the sea
Far away flashed; from fretted uplands
That lay to the north, from limestone heights
Incisive rains had dissected well,
For down each dale industrious there ran
A paternoster of ponds and mills,
Came sweet waters, assembling quietly
By a clear congress of accordant streams
A mild river that moseyed at will
Through parks and ploughland, purring southward
In a wide valley. Wolds on each side
Came dawdling downwards in double curves,
Mellow, mature, to meadowlands and
Sedentary orchards, settled places
Crowded with lives; fat cattle brooded
In the shade of great oaks, sheep grazed in
The ancient hollows of meander scars and
Long-legged ladies with little-legged dogs
Lolled with their lovers by lapsing brooks.
A couth region: consonant, lofty,
Volatile vault and vagrant buttress
Showed their shapeliness; with assured ease,
Proud on that plain, St Peter Acorn,

St Dill-in-the-Deep, St Dust, St Alb,
St Bee-le-bone, St Botolph-the-less,
High gothic growths in a grecian space,
Lorded over each leafy parish
Where country curates in cold bedrooms
Dreamed of deaneries till at day-break
The rector's rooks with relish described
Their stinted station.

EMBLE was thinking: Estranged, aloof,
They brood over being till the bars close,
The malcontented who might have been
The creative odd ones the average need
To suggest new goals. Self-judged they sit,
Sad haunters of Perhaps who after years
To grasp and gaze in get no further
Than their first beholding, phantoms who try
Through much drink by magic to restore
The primitive pact with pure feeling,
Their flesh as it felt before sex was,
(The archaic calm without cultural sin
Which her Adam is till his Eve does)
Eyeing the door, for ever expecting
Night after night the Nameless One, the
Smiling sea-god who shall safely land
Shy and broad-shouldered on the shore at last,
Enthusiastic, of their convenient

And dangerous dream; while days away, in
Prairie places where no person asks
What is suffered in ships, small tradesmen,
Wry relatives on rocking-chairs in
Moss-grown mansions, mothers whose causes
For right and wrong are unreal to them,
Grieve vaguely over theirs: their vision shrinks
As their dreams darken; with dulling voice
Each calls across a colder water,
Tense, optative, interrogating
Some sighing several who sadly fades.

But now the radio, suddenly breaking in with its banal noises upon their separate senses of themselves, by compelling them to pay attention to a common world of great slaughter and much sorrow, began, without their knowledge, to draw these four strangers closer to each other. For in response to its official doctored message:

Now the news. Night raids on
Five cities. Fires started.
Pressure applied by pincer movement
In threatening thrust. Third Division
Enlarges beachhead. Lucky charm
Saves sniper. Sabotage hinted
In steel-mill stoppage. Strong point held
By fanatical Nazis. Canal crossed

By heroic marines. Rochester barber
Fools foe. Finns ignore
Peace feeler. Pope condemns
Axis excesses. Underground
Blows up bridge. Thibetan prayer-wheels
Revolve for victory. Vital crossroads
Taken by tanks. Trend to the left
Forecast by Congressman. Cruiser sunk
In Valdivian Deep. Doomed sailors
Play poker. Reporter killed.

MALIN thought: Untalkative and tense, we took off
Anxious into air; our instruments glowed,
Dials in darkness, for dawn was not yet;
Pulses pounded; we approached our target,
Conscious in common of our closed Here
And of Them out There thinking of Us
In a different dream, for we die in theirs
Who kill in ours and become fathers
Not twisting tracks their trigger hands are
Given goals by; we began our run;
Death and damage darted at our will,
Bullets were about, blazing anger
Lunged from below, but we laid our eggs
Neatly in their nest, a nice deposit
Hatched in an instant; houses flamed in
Shuddering sheets as we shed our big

Tears on their town: we turned to come back,
But at high altitudes, hostile brains
Waited in the west, a wily flock
Vowed to vengeance in the vast morning,
—A mild morning where no marriage was,
And gravity a god greater than love—
Fierce interferers. We fought them off
But paid a price; there was pain for some.
"Why have They killed me?" wondered our Bert, our
Greenhouse gunner, forgot our answer,
Then was not with us. We watched others
Drop into death; dully we mourned each
Flare as it fell with a friend's lifetime,
While we hurried on to our home bases
To the safe smells and a sacrament
Of tea with toast. At twenty to eight I
Stepped onto grass, still with the living,
While far and near a fioritura
Of brooks and blackbirds bravely struck the
International note with no sense
Of historic truth, of time meaning
Once and for all, and my watch stuttered:—
Many have perished; more will.

And QUANT thought: All war's woes I can well imagine.
Gun-barrels glint, gathered in ambush,
Mayhem among mountains; minerals break

In by order on intimate groups of
Tender tissues; at their tough visit
Flesh flusters that was so fluent till now,
Stammers some nonsense, stops and sits down,
Apathetic to all this. Thousands lie in
Ruins by roads, irrational in woods,
Insensitive upon snow-bound plains,
Or littered lifeless along low coasts
Where shingle shuffles as shambling waves
Feebly fiddle in the fading light
With bloated bodies, beached among groynes,
Male no longer, unmotivated,
Have-beens without hopes: earth takes charge of
Soil accepts for a serious purpose
The jettisoned blood of jokes and dreams,
Making buds from bone, from brains the good
Vague vegetable; survivors play
Cards in kitchens while candles flicker
And in blood-spattered barns bandaged men,
Their poor hands in a panic of need
Groping weakly for a gun-butt or
A friendly fist, are fetched off darkling.
Many have perished; more will.

And EMBLE thought: High were those headlands; the eagles promised
Life without lawyers. Our long convoy
Turned away northward as tireless gulls

Wove over water webs of brightness
And sad sound. The insensible ocean,
Miles without mind, moaned all around our
Limited laughter, and below our songs
Were deaf deeps, denes of unaffection,
Their chill unchanging, chines where only
The whale is warm, their wildness haunted
By metal fauna moved by reason
To hunt not in hunger but for hate's sake,
Stalking our steamers. Strained with gazing
Our eyes ached, and our ears as we slept
Kept their care for the crash that would turn
Our fears into fact. In the fourth watch
A torpedo struck on the port bow:
The blast killed many; the burning oil
Suffocated some; some in lifebelts
Floated upright till they froze to death;
The younger swam but the yielding waves
Denied help; they were not supported,
They swallowed and sank, ceased thereafter
To appear in public; exposed to snap
Verdicts of sharks, to vague inquiries
Of amoeboid monsters, mobbed by slight
Unfriendly fry, refused persistence.
They are nothing now but names assigned to
Anguish in others, areas of grief.
Many have perished; more will.

ROSETTA thought: I see in my mind a besieged island,
That island in arms where my home once was.
Round green gardens, down grooves between white
Hawthorne-hedges, long hospital trains
Smoothly slide with their sensitized freight
Of mangled men, moving them homeward
In pain through pastures. In a packed hall
Two vicious rivals, two virtuosos
Appear on one platform and play duets
To war-orphans and widowed ladies,
Grieving in gloves; while to grosser ears
In clubs and cabarets crooners wail
Some miserere modern enough
In its thorough thinness. I think too of
The conquered condition, countries where
Arrogant officers, armed in cars,
Go roaring down roads on the wrong side,
Courts martial meet at midnight with drums,
And pudgy persons pace unsmiling
The quays and stations or cruise the nights
In vans for victims, to investigate
In sound-proof cells the Sense of Honor,
While in turkish baths with towels round them
Imperilled plotters plan in outline
Definitions and norms for new lives,
Half-truths for their times. As tense as these,

Four who are famous confer in a schloss
At night on nations. They are not equal:
Three stand thoughtful on a thick carpet
Awaiting the Fourth who wills they shall
Till, suddenly entering through a side-door,
Quick, quiet, unquestionable as death,
Grief or guilt, he greets them and sits down,
Lord of this life. He looks natural,
He smiles well, he smells of the future,
Odorless ages, an ordered world
Of planned pleasures and passport-control,
Sentry-go, sedatives, soft drinks and
Managed money, a moral planet
Tamed by terror: his telegram sets
Grey masses moving as the mud dries.
Many have perished; more will.

And when in conclusion the instrument said:

Buy a bond. Blood saves lives.
Donate now. Name this station.

they could no longer keep these thoughts to themselves, but turning towards each other on their high wooden stools, became acquainted.

ROSETTA
spoke first: Numbers and nightmares have news value.

Then
MALIN: A crime has occurred, accusing all.

Then
QUANT: The world needs a wash and a week's rest.

To which EMBLE said:

Better this than barbarian misrule.
History tells more often than not
Of wickedness with will, wisdom but
An interjection without a verb,
And the godless growing like green cedars
On righteous ruins. The reticent earth,
Exposed by the spade, speaks its warning
With successive layers of sacked temples
And dead civilians. They dwelt at ease
In their sown centers, sunny their minds,
Fine their features; their flesh was carried
On beautiful bones; they bore themselves
Lightly through life; they loved their children
And entertained with all their senses
A world of detail. Wave and pebble,
Boar and butterfly, birch and carp, they
Painted as persons, portraits that seem
Neighbors with names; one knows from them what
A leaf must feel. By lakes at twilight
They sang of swans and separations,
Mild, unmilitant, as the moon rose
And reeds rustled; ritual appointed
Tastes and textures; their touch preferred the
Spectrum of scents to Spartan morals,
Bells babbled in a blossoming month,
Near-sighted scholars on canal paths

Defined their terms, and fans made public
The hopes of young hearts, out of the north, from
Black tundras, from basalt and lichen,
Peripheral people, rancid ones
Stocky on horses, stomachs in need of
Game and grazing, by grass corridors
Coursed down on their concatenation
Of smiling cities. Swords and arrows
Accosted their calm; their climate knew
Fire and fear; they fell, they bled, not an
Eye was left open; all disappeared:
Utter oblivion they had after that.

MALIN said: But the new barbarian is no uncouth
Desert-dweller; he does not emerge
From fir forests: factories bred him;
Corporate companies, college towns
Mothered his mind, and many journals
Backed his beliefs. He was born here. The
Bravura of revolvers in vogue now
And the cult of death are quite at home
Inside the city.

QUANT said: The soldiers' fear
And the shots will cease in a short while,
More ruined regions surrender to less,
Prominent persons be put to death
For mass-murder, and what moves us now,

The defense of friends against foes' hate,
Be over for ever. Then, after that,
What shall we will? Why shall we practise
Vice or virtue when victory comes?
The celebrations are suddenly hushed,
The coarse crowds uncomfortably still,
For, arm-in-arm now, behind the festooned
Conqueror's car there come his heirs, the
Public hangman, the private wastrel.

ROSETTA said: Lies and lethargies police the world
In its periods of peace. What pain taught
Is soon forgotten; we celebrate
What ought to happen as if it were done,
Are blinded by our boasts. Then back they come,
The fears that we fear. We fall asleep
Only to meet the idiot children of
Our revels and wrongs; farouche they appear,
Reluctant look-behinds, loitering through
The mooing gate, menacing or smiling,
Nocturnal trivia, torts and dramas,
Wrecks, arrivals, rose-bushes, armies,
Leopards and laughs, alarming growths of
Moulds and monsters on memories stuffed
With dead men's doodles, dossiers written
In lost lingos, too long an account
To take out in trade, no time either,

Since we wake up. We are warm, our active
Universe is young; yet we shiver:
For athwart our thinking the threat looms,
Huge and awful as the hump of Saturn
Over modest Mimas, of more deaths
And worse wars, a winter of distaste
To last a lifetime. Our lips are dry, our
Knees numb; the enormous disappointment
With a smiling sigh softly flings her
Indolent apron over our lives
And sits down on our day. Damning us,
On our present purpose the past weighs
Heavy as alps, for the absent are never
Mislaid or lost: as lawyers define
The grammar of our grief, their ghosts rise,
Hanged or headless, hosts who disputed
With good governors, their guilty flesh
Racked and raving but unreconciled,
The punished people to pass sentence
On the jolly and just; and, joining these
Come worse warlocks, the wailing infants
Who know now they will never be born,
Refused a future. Our failings give
Their resentment seizin; our Zion is
A doomed Sodom dancing its heart out
To treacly tunes, a tired Gomorrah
Infatuated with her former self

Whose dear dreams though they dominate still
Are formal facts which refresh no more.

They fell silent and immediately became conscious again of the radio, now blandly inexorably bringing to all John Doakes and G.I. Joes tidings of great joy and saying

Definitely different. Has that democratic
Extra elegance. Easy to clean.
Will gladden grand-dad and your girl friend.
Lasts a lifetime. Leaves no odor.
American made. A modern product
Of nerve and know-how with a new thrill.
Patriotic to own. Is on its way
In a patent package. Pays to investigate.
Serves through science. Has something added
By skilled Scotchmen. Exclusively used
By upper classmen and Uncle Sam.
Tops in tests by teen-agers.
Just ask for it always.

Matter and manner set their teeth on edge, especially Malin's who felt like talking. So he ordered a round of drinks, then said:

Here we sit
Our bodies bound to these bar-room lights,
The night's odors, the noise of the El on
Third Avenue, but our thoughts are free . . .
Where shall they wander? To the wild past

When, beaten back, banished to their cirques
The horse-shoe glaciers curled up and died,
And cold-blooded through conifers slouched
Fumbling amphibians; forward into
Tidy utopias of eternal spring,
Vitamins, villas, visas for dogs
And art for all; or up and down through
Those hidden worlds of alien sizes
Which lenses elicit?

But EMBLE objected:

Muster no monsters, I'll meeken my own.

So did ROSETTA:

You may wish till you waste, I'll want here.

So did QUANT:

Too blank the blink of these blind heavens.

MALIN suggested:

Let us then
Consider rather the incessant Now of
The traveller through time, his tired mind
Biased towards bigness since his body must
Exaggerate to exist, possessed by hope,
Acquisitive, in quest of his own
Absconded self yet scared to find it
As he bumbles by from birth to death
Menaced by madness; whose mode of being,
Bashful or braggart, is to be at once

Outside and inside his own demand
For personal pattern. His pure I
Must give account of and greet his Me,
That field of force where he feels he thinks,
His past present, presupposing death,
Must ask what he is in order to be
And make meaning by omission and stress,
Avid of elseness. All that exists
Matters to man; he minds what happens
And feels he is at fault, a fallen soul
With power to place, to explain every
What in his world but why he is neither
God nor good, this guilt the insoluble
Final fact, infusing his private
Nexus of needs, his noted aims with
Incomprehensible comprehensive dread
At not being what he knows that before
This world was he was willed to become.

QUANT approved: Set him to song, the surly old dodger.

So did EMBLE: Relate his lies to his longing for truth.

So did ROSETTA: Question his crimes till his clues confess.

The radio attempted to interrupt by remarking

And now Captain Kidd in his Quiz Programme
HOW ALERT ARE YOU

But Quant pointed a finger at it and it stopped immediately. He said:

Listen, Box,
And keep quiet. Listen courteously to us
Four reformers who have founded—why not?—
The Gung-Ho Group, the Ganymede Club
For homesick young angels, the Arctic League
Of Tropical Fish, the Tomboy Fund
For Blushing Brides and the Bide-a-wees
Of Sans-Souci, assembled again
For a Think-Fest: our theme tonight is

HOMO ABYSSUS OCCIDENTALIS

or

A CURIOUS CASE OF COLD FEET

or

SEVEN SELFISH SUPPERLESS AGES

And now, at Rosetta's suggestion, they left their bar-stools and moved to the quieter intimacy of a booth. Drinks were ordered and the discussion began.

PART TWO

THE SEVEN AGES

A sick toss'd vessel, dashing on each thing;
Nay, his own shelf:
My God, I mean myself.
George Herbert *Miserie*

MALIN began:

Behold the infant, helpless in cradle and
Righteous still, yet already there is
Dread in his dreams at the deed of which
He knows nothing but knows he can do,
The gulf before him with guilt beyond,
Whatever that is, whatever why
Forbids his bound; till that ban tempts him;
He jumps and is judged: he joins mankind,
The fallen families, freedom lost,
Love become Law. Now he looks at grown-ups
With conscious care, and calculates on
The effect of a frown or filial smile,
Accuses with a cough, claims pity
With scratched knees, skillfully avenges
Pains and punishments on puny insects,
Grows into a grin, and gladly shares his
Small secret with the supplicating
Instant present. His emptiness finds
Its joy in a gang and is joined to others

By crimes in common. Clumsy and alarmed,
As the blind bat obeys the warnings
Of its own echoes, his inner life
Is a zig-zag, a bizarre dance of
Feelings through facts, a foiled one learning
Shyness and shame, a shadowed flier.

QUANT said:

O
Secret meetings at the slaughter-house
With nickels and knives, initiations
Behind the billboards. Then the hammerpond looked
So green and grim, yet graciously its dank
Water made us welcome—once in, we
Swam without swearing. The smelting mill
We broke into had a big chimney
And huge engines; holding our breath, we
Lighted matches and looked at the gears,
The cruel cogwheels, the crank's absolute
Veto on pleasure. In a vacant lot
We built a bonfire and burned alive
Some stolen tires. How strong and good one
Felt at first, how fagged coming home through
The urban evening. Heavy like us
Sank the gas-tanks—it was supper time.
In hot houses helpless babies and
Telephones gabbled untidy cries,
And on embankments black with burnt grass

Shambling freight-trains were shunted away
Past crimson clouds.

EMBLE said:

My cousins were both
Strong and stupid: they stole my candy,
They tied me to a tree, they twisted my arms,
Called me crybaby. "Take care," I sobbed,
"I could hold up my hand and hot water
Would come down on your drought and drown you all
In your big boots." In our back garden
One dark afternoon I dug quite a hole
Planning to vanish.

ROSETTA said:

On picnic days
My dearest doll was deaf and spoke in
Grunts like grandfather. God understood
If we washed our necks he wasn't ever
To look in the loft where the Lamps were
And the Holy Hook. In the housekeeper's room there
Was currant cake and calves-foot jelly
As we did our sums while down below,
Tall in tweeds on the terrace gravel,
Father and his friends reformed régimes,
Monies and monarchs, and mother wrote
Swift and sure in the silk-hung saloon
Her large round letters. Along the esker,

Following a fox with our fingers crossed
Or after the ogre in Indian file,
We stole with our sticks through a still world of
Hilarious light, our lives united
Like fruit in a bowl, befriended by
The supple silence, incited by
Our shortened shadows.

Malin went on to the Second Age:

With shaving comes
An hour when he halts, hearing the crescent
Roar of hazard, and realizes first
He has laid his life-bet with a lying self
Who wins or welches. Thus woken, he is
Amused no more by a merely given
Felt fact, the facile emergence of
Thought with thing, but, threatened from all sides,
Embarrassed by his body's bald statements,
His sacred soul obscenely tickled
And bellowed at by a blatant Without,
A dog by daylight, in dreams a lamb
Whom the nightmare ejects nude into
A ball of princes too big to feel
Disturbed by his distress, he starts off now,
Poor, unprepared, on his pilgrimage
To find his friends, the far-off élite,

And, knowing no one, a nameless young man,
Pictures as he plods his promised chair
In their small circle secret to those
With no analogies, unique persons,
The originals' ring, the round table
Of master minds. Mountains he loves now,
Piers and promontories, places where
Evening brings him all that grandeur
Of scope and scale which the sky is believed
To promise or recall, pacing by
In a sunset trance of self-pity
While his toy tears with a touching grace
Like little balloons sail lonely away
To dusk and death.

QUANT said:

With diamonds to offer,
A cleaned tycoon in a cooled office,
I smiled at a siren with six breasts,
Leaning on leather, looking up at
Her righteous robber, her Robin Hood,
Her plump prince. All the public could see
Was a bus-boy brushing a table,
Sullen and slight.

ROSETTA said:

In my sixteenth year
Before sleeping I fancied nightly
The house on the headland I would own one day.

Its long windows overlooked the sea
And its turf terrace topped a sunny
Sequestered cove. A corkscrew staircase
From a green gate in the garden wall
Descended the cliff, the sole entrance
To my beach where bathers basked beside
The watchet waves. Though One was special,
All forms were friends who freely told their
Secrets to me; but, safe in my purse
I kept the key to the closet where
A sliding panel concealed the lift,
Known to none, which at night would take me
Down through the dark to my dock below,
A chamber chiselled in the chalk hill,
Private and perfect; thence, putting forth
Alone in my launch through a low tunnel
Out to the ocean, while all others slept,
Smiling and singing I sailed till dawn,
Happy, hatless.

EMBLE said:

After a dreadful
Row with father, I ran with burning
Cheeks to the pasture and chopped wood, my
Stomach like a stone. I strode that night
Through wicked dreams: waking, I skipped to
The shower and sang, ashamed to recall
With whom or how; the hiss of the water

Composed the tune, I supplied the words
For a fine dirge which fifty years hence
Massed choirs would sing as my coffin passed,
Grieved for and great on a gun-carriage.

Malin went on, spoke of the Third Age:

Such pictures fade as his path is blocked
By Others from Elsewhere, alien bodies
Whose figures fasten on his free thoughts,
Ciphers and symbols secret to his flesh,
Uniquely near, needing his torments,
His lonely life, and he learns what real
Images are; that, however violent
Their wish to be one, that wild promise
Cannot be kept, their case is double;
For each now of need ignores the other as
By rival routes of recognition
Diminutive names that midnight hears
Intersect upon their instant way
To solid solitudes, and selves cross
Back to bodies, both insisting each
Proximate place a pertinent thing.
So, learning to love, at length he is taught
To know he does not.

QUANT said: Since the neighbors did,
With a multitude I made the long
Visitors' voyage to Venus Island,

Elated as they, landed upon
That savage shore where old swains lay wrecked
Unfit for her fable, followed up
The basalt stairway bandying jokes with
The thoughtless throng, but then, avoiding
The great gate where she gives all pilgrims
Her local wine, I legged it over
A concrete wall, was cold sober as,
Pushing through brambles, I peeked out at
Her fascination. Frogs were shooting
Craps in a corner; cupids on stilts,
Their beautiful bottoms breaking wind,
Hunted hares with hurricane lanterns
Through woods on one side, while on the other,
Shining out through shivering poplars,
Stood a brick bath-house where burghers mixed
With light-fingered ladies and louche trade,
Dancing in serpents and daisy chains
To mad music. In the mid-distance
On deal chairs sat a dozen decayed
Gentlewomen with dejected backs
And raw fingers morosely stitching
Red flannel scivvies for heroic herms.
Primroses, peacocks and peachtrees made
A fair foreground but fairer there, with
An early Madonna's oval face
And lissom limbs, delighting that whole

Degraded glen, the Goddess herself
Presided smiling; a saucy wind,
Plucking from her thigh her pink wrapper
Of crêpe-de-chine, disclosed a very
Indolent ulcer.

Rosetta said nothing but, placing a nickel in the Wallomatic, selected a sad little tune *The Case Is Closed* (*Tschaikovsky—Fink*) and sang to it softly:

Deep in my dark the dream shines
Yes, of you, you dear always;
My cause to cry, cold but my
Story still, still my music.

Mild rose the moon, moving through our
Naked nights: tonight it rains;
Black umbrellas blossom out;
Gone the gold, my golden ball.

Heavy these hands. I believed
That pleased pause, your pause was me
To love alone till life's end:
I thought this; this was not true.

You touched, you took. Tears fall. O
Fair my far, when far ago
Like waterwheels wishes spun
Radiant robes: but the robes tore.

Emble did likewise but his choice was a hot number, *Bugs in the Bed* by *Bog Myrtle & Her Two-Timers.* He sang gaily:

His Queen was forward, Her King was shy;
He hoped for Her Heart but He overbid;
When She ducked His Diamond down They went.

In Smuggler's Cove He smelt near Him
Her musical mermaids; She met His angels
In Locksmith's Lane, the little dears.

He said to Her: "You're a hazy truth;"
She said to Him: "You're a shining lie;"
Each went to a washroom and wept much.

The public applauded and the poets drew
A moral for marriage: "The moths will get you
If the wolves won't, so why not now?"

The consequence was Both claimed the insurance
And the furniture gave what-for to Their elbows.
A reason for One, a risk on the Pair.

Malin went on, spoke of the Fourth Age:

Now unreckoned with, rough, his road descends
From the haughty and high, the humorless places

His dreams would prefer, and drops him till,
As his forefathers did, he finds out
Where his world lies. By the water's edge,
The unthinking flood, down there, yes, is his
Proper place, the polychrome Oval
With its kleig lights and crowd engineers,
The mutable circus where mobs rule
The arena with roars, the real world of
Theology and horses, our home because
In that doubt-condemning dual kingdom
Signs and insignia decide our cause,
Fanatics of the Egg or Knights sworn to
Die for the Dolphin, and our deeds wear
Heretic green or orthodox blue,
Safe and certain.

ROSETTA said:

Too soon we embrace that
Impermanent appetitive flux,
Humorous and hard, which adults fear
Is real and right, the irreverent place,
The clown's cosmos.

EMBLE said:

Who is comforted by it?
Pent in the packed compulsory ring
Round father's frown each *famus* waits his
Day to dominate. Here a dean sits
Making bedroom eyes at a beef steak,

As wholly oral as the avid creatures
Of the celibate sea; there, sly and wise
Commuters mimic the Middle Way,
Trudging on time to a tidy fortune.
(A senator said: "From swimming-hole
To board-meeting is a big distance.")
Financiers on knolls, noses pointing
East towards oil fields, inhale the surplus
Their bowels boast of, while boys and girls, their
Hot hearts covered over with marriage
To tyrant functions, turn by degrees
To cold fish, though, precarious on the
Fringes of their feeling, a fuzzy hope
Persists somehow that sometime all this
Will walk away, and a wish gestates
For explosive pain, a punishing
Demanded moment of mortal change,
The Night of the Knock when none shall sleep,
The Absolute Instant.

QUANT said: It is here, now.
For the huge wild beast of the Unexpected
Leaps on the lax recollecting back;
Unknown to him, binoculars follow
The leaping lad; lightning at noonday
Swiftly stooping to the summer-house
Engraves its disgust on engrossed flesh,

And at tea-times through tall french windows
Hurtle anonymous hostile stones.
No soul is safe. Let slight infection
Disturb a trifle some tiny gland,
And Caustic Keith grows kind and silly
Or Dainty Daisy dirties herself.
We are mocked by unmeaning; among us fall
Aimless arrows, hurting at random
As we plan to pain.

Malin went on, spoke of the Fifth Age:

In peace or war,
Married or single, he muddles on,
Offending, fumbling, falling over,
And then, rather suddenly, there he is
Standing up, an astonished victor
Gliding over the good glib waters
Of the social harbor to set foot
On its welcoming shore where at last
Recognition surrounds his days with
Her felicitous light. He likes that;
He fairly blooms; his fever almost
Relaxes its hold. He learns to speak
Softer and slower, not to seem so eager;
His body acquires the blander motions
Of the approved state. His positive glow
Of fiscal health affects that unseen

Just judge, that Generalized Other
To whom he thinks and is understood by,
Who grows less gruff as if gravely impressed
By his evident air of having now
Really arrived, bereaved of every
Low relation.

EMBLE said: Why leave out the worst
Pang of youth? The princes of fiction,
Who ride through risks to rescue their loves,
Know their business, are not really
As young as they look. To be young means
To be all on edge, to be held waiting in
A packed lounge for a Personal Call
From Long Distance, for the low voice that
Defines one's future. The fears we know
Are of not knowing. Will nightfall bring us
Some awful order—Keep a hardware store
In a small town. . . . Teach science for life to
Progressive girls—? It is getting late.
Shall we ever be asked for? Are we simply
Not wanted at all?

QUANT said: Well, you will soon
Not bother but acknowledge yourself
As market-made, a commodity
Whose value varies, a vendor who has

To obey his buyer, will embrace moreover
The problems put you by opposing time,
The fight with work, the feud of marriage,
Whose detonating details day and night
Invest your breathing and veto sleep,
As their own answers, like others find
The train-ride between your two natures,
The morning-evening moment when
You are free to reflect on your faults still,
Is an awkward hiatus, is indeed
The real risk to be read away with
Print and pictures, reports of what should
Never have happened, will no longer
Expect more pattern, more purpose than
Your finite fate.

ROSETTA said: I refuse to accept
Your plain place, your unprivileged time.
No. No. I shall not apologize
Nor retire contempt for this tawdry age.
The juke-box jives rejoicing madly
As life after life lapses out of
Its essential self and sinks into
One press-applauded public untruth
And, massed to its music, all march in step
Led by that liar, the lukewarm Spirit
Of the Escalator, ever timely,

His whims their will, away from freedom
To a locker-room life at low tension,
Abnormal none, anonymous hosts
Driven like Danaids by drill sergeants
To ply well-paid repetitive tasks
(Dowdy they'll die who have so dimly lived)
In cosy crowds. Till the caring poet,
Child of his chamber, chooses rightly
His pleased picture of pure solitudes
Where gusts gamble over gaunt areas
Frozen and futile but far enough
From vile civilities vouched for by
Statisticians, this stupid world where
Gadgets are gods and we go on talking,
Many about much, but remain alone,
Alive but alone, belonging—where?—
Unattached as tumbleweed. Time flies.

QUANT said: No, Time returns, a continuous Now
As the clock counts. The captain sober
Gulps his beer as the galley-boy drunk
Gives away his water; William East is
Entering Olive as Alfred West
Is leaving Elaine; Lucky McGuire
Divides the spoil as Vacuous Molly
Joins in the joke; Justice van Diemen
Foresees the day when the slaves rise and

Ragamuffins roll around the block
His cone-shaped skull while Convict 90
Remembers his mother. We move on
As the wheel wills; one revolution
Registers all things, the rise and fall
In pay and prices, peregrinations
Of lies and loves, colossal bangs and
Their sequential quiets in quick order.
And who runs may read written on walls
Eternal truths: "Teddy Peterson
Never washes." "I'm not your father
You slobbering Swede." "Sulky Moses
Has bees in his bush." "Betty is thinner
But Connie lays."—Who closes his eyes
Sees the blonde vistas bathed in sunlight,
The temples, tombs, and terminal god,
Tall by a torrent, the etruscan landscape
Of Man's Memory. His myths of Being
Are there always. In that unchanging
Lucid lake where he looks for ever
Narcissus sees the sensitive face
He's too intelligent to trust or like
Pleading his pardon. Polyphemus
Curses his cave or, catching a nymph,
Begs for brotherhood with a big stick,
Hobbledehoy and helpless. Kind Orpheus lies
Violently slain on the virid bank,

That smooth sward where he sinned against
kind,
And, wild by the water, women stone
The broken torso but the bloody head,
In the far distance, floating away
Down the steady stream, still opening
Its charming mouth, goes chanting on in
Fortissimo tones, a tenor lyre
Dinning the doom into a deaf Nature
Of her loose chaos. For Long-Ago has been
Ever-After since Ur-Papa gave
The Primal Yawn that expressed all things
(In His Boredom their beings) and brought forth
The wit of this world. One-Eye's mistake
Is sorry He spoke.

Malin went on, spoke of the Sixth Age:

Our subject has changed.
He looks far from well; he has fattened on
His public perch; takes pills for vigor
And sound sleep, and sees in his mirror
The jawing genius of a jackass age,
A rich bore. When he recollects his
Designed life, the presented pomp is
A case of chaos, a constituted
Famine of effect. Feverish in
Their bony building his brain cells keep

Their hectic still, but his heart transfixed
By the ice-splinter of an ingrown tear,
Comatose in her cave, cares little
What the senses say; at the same time,
Dedicated, clandestine under
The guilt and grime of a great career,
The bruise of his boyhood is as blue still,
Horrid and hurting, hostile to his life
As a praised person. He pines for some
Nameless Eden where he never was
But where in his wishes once again
On hallowed acres, without a stitch
Of achievement on, the children play
Nor care how comely they couldn't be
Since they needn't know they're not happy.

QUANT said: So do the ignored. In the soft-footed
Hours of darkness when elevators
Raise blondes aloft to bachelor suites
And the night-nurse notices a change
In the patient's breathing, and Pride lies
Awake in himself too weak to stir
As Shame and Regret shove into his their
Inflamed faces, we failures inquire
For the treasure also. I too have shed
The tears of parting at Traitor's Halt
Where comforts finished and kind but dull,

In low landaus and electric broughams,
Through wrought-iron gates, down rhododendron
Avenues they came, Sir Ambrose Touch,
Fat Lady Feel, Professor Howling,
Doctor Dort, dear Mrs. Pollybore,
And the Scarsdale boy with a school friend
To see us off. (But someone important,
Alas, was not there.) Some laughed of course.
Ha-ha, ha-ha, cried Hairy Mary
The lighthouse lady, little Miss Odd,
And Will Walton the watercress man,
And pointed northward. Repellent there
A storm was brewing, but we started out
In carpet-slippers by candlelight
Through Wastewood in the wane of the year,
Past Torture Tower and Twisting Ovens,
Their ruins ruled by the arrested insect
And abortive bird. In the bleak dawn
We reached Red River; on Wrynose Weir
Lay a dead salmon; when the dogs got wind
They turned tail. We talked very little;
Thunder thudded; on the thirteenth day
Our diseased guide deserted with all
The milk chocolate. Emerging from
Forests to foothills, our fears increased,
For roads grew rougher and ridges were

Congested with gibbets. We had just reached
The monastery bridge; the mist cleared;
I got one glimpse of the granite walls
And the glaciers guarding the Good Place.
(A giant jawbone jutted from that ice;
Condors on those crags coldly observed our
Helpless anguish.) My hands in my pockets,
Whistling ruefully I wandered back
By Maiden Moor and Mockbeggar Lane
To Nettlenaze where nightingales sang
Of my own evil.

ROSETTA said: Yet holy are the dolls
Who, junior for ever, just begin
Their open lives in absolute space,
Are simply themselves, deceiving none,
Their clothes creatures, so clearly expressing,
Tearless, timeless, the paternal world
Of pillars and parks. O Primal Age
When we danced deisal, our dream-wishes
Vert and volant, unvetoed our song.
For crows brought cups of cold water to
Ewes that were with young; unicorn herds
Galumphed through lilies; little mice played
With great cock-a-hoop cats; courteous griffins
Waltzed with wyverns, and the wild horses

Drew nigh their neighbors and neighed with joy,
All feasting with friends. What faded you
To this drab dusk? O the drains are clogged,
Rain-rusted, the roofs of the privies
Have fallen in, the flag is covered
With stale stains and the stable-clock face
Mottled with moss. Mocking blows the wind
Into my mouth. O but they've left me.
I wronged. Then they ran. I'm running down.
Wafna. Wafna. Who's to wind me now
In this lost land?

EMBLE said: I've lost the key to
The garden gate. How green it was there,
How large long ago when I looked out,
Excited by sand, the sad glitter
Of desert dreck, not dreaming I saw
My future home. It foils my magic:
Right is the ritual but wrong the time,
The place improper.

QUANT said: Reproaches come,
Emanating from some hidden center,
Cold radiations directed at us
In waves unawares, and we are shaken
By a sceptical sigh from a scotch fir,
The Accuser crying in a cocktail glass.

Someone had put on the juke box a silly number *With That Thing* as played by *The Three Snorts,* and to this he sang:

Let me sell you a song, the most side-splitting tale
Since old Chaos caught young Cosmos bending
With his back bare and his braces down,
Homo Vulgaris, the Asterisk Man.

He burned all his boats and both pink ends
Of his crowing candle, cooked his goose-flesh,
Jumped his bailiwick, jilted his heirs
And pickled his piper, the Approximate Man.

With his knees to the north and the night in his stride
He advanced on the parlors, then vanished upstairs
As a bath-tub admiral to bark commands
At his ten hammer toes, the Transient Man.

Once in his while his wit erupted
One pure little puff, one pretty idea;
A fumerole since he has fizzled a cloud
Of gossip and gas, the Guttering Man.

Soon his soul will be sent up to Secret Inks,
His body be bought by the Breakdown Gang;

It's time for the Ticklers to take him away
In a closed cab, the Camouflage Man.

So look for a laundress to lay him out cold,
A fanciful fairy to fashion his tomb
In Rest-room Roman; get ready to pray
In a wheel-chair voice for the Watery Man.

Malin went on once more, spoke of the Seventh Age:

His last chapter has little to say.
He grows backward with gradual loss of
Muscular tone and mental quickness:
He lies down; he looks through the window
Ailing at autumn, asks a sign but
The afternoons are inert, none come to
Quit his quarrel or quicken the long
Years of yawning and he yearns only
For total extinction. He is tired out;
His last illusions have lost patience
With the human enterprise. The end comes: he
Joins the majority, the jaw-dropped
Mildewed mob and is modest at last.
There his case rests: let who can disprove.

So their discussion concluded. Malin excused himself and went to the men's room. Quant went to the bar to fetch more drinks. Rosetta and Emble sat silent, occupied with memories of a distant or recent, a real or imaginary past.

ROSETTA was thinking:

There was Lord Lugar at Lighthazels,
Violent-tempered; he voted against
The Banking Bill. At Brothers Intake
Sir William Wand; his Water Treaty
Enriched Arabia. At Rotherhope
General Locke, a genial man who
Kept cormorants. At Craven Ladies
Old Tillingham-Trench; he had two passions,
Women and walking-sticks. At Wheels Rake,
In his low library loving Greek
Bishop Bottrel; he came back from the East
With a fat notebook full of antique
Liturgies and laws, long-forgotten
Christian creeds occluded within a
Feldspar fortress. Fay was his daughter;
A truant mutation, she took up art,
Carved in crystal, became the friend of
Green-eyed Gelert the great dressmaker,
And died in Rome. There was Dr. Sykes
At Mugglers Mound; his monograph on
The chronic cough is a classic still;
He was loved by all. At Lantern Byepew
Susan O'Rourke, a sensitive who
Prayed for the plants. They have perished now; their
Level lawns and logical vistas
Are obliterated; their big stone

Houses are shut. Ease is rejected,
Poor and penalized the private state.

EMBLE was thinking:

I have friends already, faces I know
In that calm crowd, wearing clothes like mine,
Who have settled down, accepted at once,
Contemporary with Trojan Knights
And Bronze-Age bagmen; Bud and Whitey
And Clifford Monahan and Clem Lifschutz,
Dicky Lamb, Dominic Moreno,
Svensson, Seidel: they seem already
Like anyone else. Must I end like that?

Waiting to be served, Quant caught sight of himself again in the bar mirror and thought:

Ingenious George reached his journey's end
Killed by a cop in a comfort station,
Dan dropped dead at his dinner table,
Mrs. O'Malley with Miss De Young
Wandered away into wild places
Where desert dogs reduced their status
To squandered bones, and it's scared you look,
Dear friend of a friend, to face me now.
How limply you've aged, how loose you stand
A frog in your fork, my far-away
Primrose prince, but a passenger here
Retreating to his tent. Whose trump hails your

Shenanigans now? Kneel to your bones
And cuddle your cough. Your castle's down.
It rains as you run, rusts where you lie.
Beware my weakness. Worse will follow.
The Blue Little Boys should blow their horns
Louder and longer, for the lost sheep
Are nibbling nightshade. But never mind . . .

Malin returned and Quant brought back drinks to the table. Then raising his glass to Rosetta, Quant said:

Come, peregrine nymph, display your warm
Euphoric flanks in their full glory
Of liberal life; with luscious note
Smoothly sing the softer data of an
Unyielding universe, youth, money,
Liquor and love; delight your shepherds
For crazed we come and coarsened we go
Our wobbling way: there's a white silence
Of antiseptics and instruments
At both ends, but a babble between
And a shame surely. O show us the route
Into hope and health; give each the required
Pass to appease the superior archons;
Be our good guide.

To which ROSETTA answered:

What gift of direction
Is entrusted to me to take charge
Of an expedition any may

Suggest or join? For the journey homeward
Arriving by roads already known
At sites and sounds one has sensed before,
The knowledge needed is not special,
The sole essential a sad unrest
Which no life can lack. Long is the way
Of the Seven Stages, slow the going,
And few, maybe, are faithful to the end,
But all start out with the hope of success,
Arm in arm with their opposite type
Like dashing Adonis dressed to kill
And worn Wat with his walrus moustache,
Or one by one like Wandering Jews,
Bullet-headed bandit, broad churchman,
Lobbyist, legatee, loud virago,
Uncle and aunt and alien cousin,
Mute or maddening through the Maze of Time,
Seek its center, desiring like us
The Quiet Kingdom. Comfort your wills then
With hungry hopes; to this indagation
Allay your longings: may our luck find the
Regressive road to Grandmother's House.

As everyone knows, many people reveal in a state of semi-intoxication capacities which are quite beyond them when they are sober: the shy talk easily and brilliantly to total strangers, the stammerers get through complicated sentences without a bitch, the unathletic is translated into a weight-lifter or a sprinter, the prosaic show an intuitive grasp of myth and symbol. A less noted and a more significant phenomenon, however, is the way in which our faith in the existence of other selves, normally rather wobbly, is greatly strengthened and receives, perhaps precisely because, for once, doubt is so completely overcome, the most startling justifications. For it can happen, if circumstances are otherwise propitious, that members of a group in this condition establish a rapport in which communication of thoughts and feelings is so accurate and instantaneous, that they appear to function as a single organism.

So it was now as they sought that state of prehistoric happiness which, by human beings, can only be imagined in terms of a landscape bearing a symbolic resemblance to the human body. The more completely these four forgot their surroundings and lost their sense of time, the more sensitively aware of each other they became, until they achieved in their dream that rare community which is otherwise only attained in states of extreme wakefulness. But this did not happen all at once.

PART THREE

THE SEVEN STAGES

O Patria, patria! Quanto mi costi!
A. Ghislanzoni *Aida*

At first all is dark and each walks alone. What they share is only the feeling of remoteness and desertion, of having marched for miles and miles, of having lost their bearings, of a restless urge to find water. Gradually for each in turn the darkness begins to dissolve and their vision to take shape.

Quant is the first to see anything. He says:

Groping through fog, I begin to hear
A salt lake lapping:
Dotterels and dunlins on its dark shores
Scurry this way and that.

Now Rosetta perceives clearly and says:

In the center of a sad plain
Without forests or footpaths,
Rimmed with rushes and moss
I see a tacit tarn.

Some oddling angler in summer
May visit the spot, or a spy
Come here to cache a stolen
Map or meet a rival.

But who remarks the beehive mounds,
Graves of creatures who cooked
And wanted to be worshipped and perhaps
Were the first to feel our sorrow?

And now MALIN: How still it is; the horses
Have moved into the shade, the mothers
Have followed their migrating gardens.

Curlews on kettle moraines
Foretell the end of time,
The doom of paradox

But lovelorn sighs ascend
From wretched greedy regions
Which cannot include themselves.

And the freckled orphan flinging
Ducks and drakes at the pond
Stops looking for stones,

And wishes he were a steamboat,
Or Lugalzaggisi the loud
Tyrant of Erech and Umma.

And last EMBLE: The earth looks woeful and wet;
On the raw horizon regiments pass
Tense against twilight, tired beneath
Their corresponsive spears.

Slogging on through slush
By broken bridges and burnt hamlets
Where the starving stand, staring past them
At remote inedible hills.

And now, though separate still, they begin to advance from their several starting-points into the same mountainous district. Rosetta says:

Now peaks oppose to the ploughman's march
Their twin confederate forms,
In a warm weather, white with lilies,
Evergreen for grazing.

Smooth the surfaces, sweeping the curves
Of these comely frolic clouds,
Where the great go to forget themselves,
The beautiful and boon to die.

QUANT says:

Lights are moving
On the domed hills
Where the little monks
Get up in the dark.

Though wild volcanoes
Growl in their sleep
At the green world,
Inside their cloisters

They sit translating
A vision into
The vulgar lingo
Of armed cities,

Where brides arrive
Through great doors
And robbers' bones
Dangle from gallows.

EMBLE says:

Bending forward
With stern faces,
Pilgrims puff
Up the steep bank
In huge hats.

Shouting I run
In the other direction,
Cheerful, unchaste,
With open shirt
And tinkling guitar.

MALIN says:

Looming over my head
Mountains menace my life,
But on either hand, let down
From U-valleys like yarn,
Waterfalls all the way
Quietly encourage me on.

And now one by one they enter the same valley and begin to ascend the same steep pass. Rosetta is in front, then Emble, then Malin and Quant last.

ROSETTA says: These hills may be hollow; I've a horror of dwarfs
And a streaming cold.

EMBLE says: This stony pass
Is bad for my back. My boots are too small
My haversack too heavy. I hate my knees
But like my legs.

MALIN says: The less I feel
The more I mind. I should meet death
With great regret.

QUANT says: Thank God I was warned
To bring an umbrella and had bribes enough
For the red-haired rascals, for the reservoir guard
A celluloid sandwich, and silk eggs
For the lead smelters; for Lizzie O'Flynn,
The capering cowgirl with clay on her hands,
Tasty truffles in utopian jars,
And dungarees with Danish buttons
For Shilly and Shally the shepherd kings.

Now ROSETTA says: The ground's aggression is growing less.
The clouds are clearing.

EMBLE says: My cape is dry.
I can reckon correctly.

MALIN says: My real intentions
Are nicer now.

And QUANT says: I'm nearing the top.
When I hear what I'm up to, how I shall laugh.

And so, on a treeless watershed, at the tumbledown Mariners Tavern (which is miles inland) the four assemble, having completed the first stage of their journey. They look about them, and everything seems somehow familiar. Emble says:

The railroads like the rivers run for the most part
East and west, and from here
On a clear day both coasts are visible
And the long piers of their ports.
To the south one sees the sawtooth range
Our nickel and copper come from,
And beyond it the Barrens used for Army
Manœuvres; while to the north

A brown blur of buildings marks
Some sacred or secular town.

MALIN says:

Every evening the oddest collection
Of characters crowd this inn:
Here a face from a farm, its frankness yearning
For corruption and riches; there
A gaunt gospel whom grinning miners
Will stone to death by a dolmen;
Heroes confess to whores, detectives
Chat or play chess with thieves.

QUANT says:

And one finds it hard to fall asleep here.
Lying awake and listening
To the creak of new creeds on the kitchen stairs
Or the sob of a dream next door,
(By pass and port they percolated,
By friendships and official channels)
Gentler grows the heart, gentler and much
Less certain it will succeed.

But ROSETTA says impatiently:

Questioned by these crossroads our common hope
Replies we must part; in pairs proceed
By bicycle, barge, or bumbling local,
As vagabonds or in wagon-lits,
On weedy waters, up winding lanes,
Down rational roads the Romans built,

Over or into, under or round
Mosses dismal or mountains sudden,
Farmlands or fenlands or factory towns,
Left and right till the loop be complete
And we meet once more.

EMBLE whispers to himself: Do I mind with whom?
Yes, a great deal.

And MALIN: In youth I would have cared,
But not now.

And QUANT: I know what will happen,
Am sincerely sorry.

They divide thus, youth with youth and age with age. To the left go Rosetta and Emble, to the right Quant and Malin, these on foot, those by car, moving outwards in opposite directions from the high heartland to the maritime plains.

EMBLE says: As I pull on my gloves and prepare
For another day-long drive,
The landscape is full of life:
Nieces of millionaires
Twitter on terraces,

Peasant wives are pounding
Linen on stones by a stream,
And a doctor's silk hat dances
On top of a hedge as he hurries
Along a sunken lane.

All these and theirs are at home,
May love or hate their age
And the beds they are built to fit;
Only I have no work
But my endless journey, its joy
The whirr of wheels, the hiss
As moonlit miles flash by,
Its grief the glimpse of a face
Whose unique beauty cannot
Be asked to alter with me.

Or must everyone see himself
As I, as the pilgrim prince
Whose life belongs to his quest
For the Truth, the tall princess,
The buried gold or the Grail,
The important thought-of Thing
Which is never here and now
Like this world through which he goes
That all the others appear
To possess the secret of?

QUANT says: Between pollarded poplars
This rural road
Ambles downhill
In search of the sea.

Nothing, neither
The farms nor the flowers,
The cows nor the clouds,
Look restive or wrong.

Then why without warning,
In my old age,
My duty done,
Do I change to a child,

And shake with shame,
Afraid of Father,
Demanding Mother's
Forgiveness again?

ROSETTA says: The light collaborates with a land of ease,
And rivers meander at random
Through meadowsweet massed on moist pastures,
Past decrepit palaces
Where, brim from belvederes, bred for riding
And graceful dancing, gaze
Fine old families who fear dishonor.

But modern on the margin of marshy ground
Glitter the glassier homes

Of more practical people with plainer minds,
And along the vacationer's coast,
Distributed between its hotels and casinos,
Ex-monarchs remember a past
Of wars and waltzes as they wait for death.

MALIN says: Though dunes still hide from the eye
The shining shore,
Already by a certain exciting
Kind of discomfort
I know the ocean near.

For wind and whining gull
Are saying something,
Or trying to say, about time
And the anxious heart
Which a matter-snob would dismiss.

So, arriving two and two at the rival ports, they complete the second stage of their journey.

ROSETTA says: These ancient harbors are hailed by the morning
Light that untidies
Warehouses and wharves and wilder rocks
Where intolerant lives
Fight and feed in the fucoid thickets
Of popular pools.

EMBLE says: Reflected fleets, feeling in awe
Of their sheltered lagoons,
Stand still, a steady congregation
Of gigantic shadows;
Derricks on these docks adore in silence
The noon they denote.

MALIN says: Quiet falls the dusk at this queasy juncture
Of water and earth,
And lamps are lit on the long esplanade;
Urgent whispers
Promise peace, and impatience shakes
Ephemeral flesh.

And QUANT says: As, far from furniture and formal gardens
The desperate spirit
Thinks of its end in the third person,
As a speck drowning
In those wanton mansions where the whales take
Their huge fruitions.

But here they may not linger long. Emble says to Rosetta:

A private plane, its propeller tied
With red ribbons is ready waiting
To take us to town.

MALIN says to QUANT: A train whistles
For the last time. We must leave at once.

And so by air, by rail, they turn inland again towards a common goal.

QUANT says:

Autumn has come early; evening falls;
Our train is traversing at top speed
A pallid province of puddles and stumps
Where helpless objects, an orphaned quarry,
A waif of a works, a widowed engine,
For a sorry second sigh and are gone
As we race through the rain with rattling windows
Bound for a borough all bankers revere.

ROSETTA says:

Lulled by an engine's hum,
Our insulated lives
Go floating freely through
Space in a metal spore.

White hangs the waning moon,
A scruple on the sky,
And constellations crowd
Our neighborhood the night.

QUANT says:

In the smoking cars all seats are taken
By melancholics mewed in their dumps,
Elegant old-school ex-lieutenants
Cashiered for shuddering, short blowhards,
Thwarted geniuses in threadbare coats,

Once well-to-do's at their wits' end,
And underpaid agents of underground powers
The faded and failing in flight towards town.

ROSETTA says:
Just visible but vague,
Way down below us lies
The world of hares and hounds,
Open to our contempt.

Escaping by our skill
Its public prison, we
Could love ourselves and live
In just anarchic joy.

QUANT says:
The parlor cars and Pullmans are packed also
With scented assassins, salad-eaters
Who murder on milk, merry expressives,
Pert pyknics with pumpkin heads,
Clever cardinals with clammy hands,
Jolly logicians with juvenile books,
Farmers, philistines, filles-de-joie,
The successful smilers the city can use.

ROSETTA says:
What fear of freedom then
Causes our clasping hands
To make in miniature
That earth anew, and now

By choice instead of chance
To suffer from the same
Attraction and untruth,
Suspicion and respect?

QUANT says: What mad oracle could have made us believe
The capital will be kind when the country is not,
And value our vanities, provide our souls
With play and pasture and permanent water?

They lose altitude, they slow down, they arrive at the city, having completed the third stage of the journey, and are united once more, greet each other.

EMBLE says: Here we are.

MALIN says: As we hoped we have come
Together again.

ROSETTA says: I am glad, I think.
It is fun to be four.

QUANT says: The flushed animations
Of crowds and couples look comic to friends.

They look about them with great curiosity. Then Malin says:

The scene has all the signs of a facetious culture,
Publishing houses, pawnshops and pay-toilets;

August and Graeco-Roman are the granite
temples
Of the medicine men whose magic keeps this body
Politic free from fevers,
Cancer and constipation.

The rooms near the railroad-station are rented
mainly
By the criminally inclined; the Castle is open
on Sundays;
There are parks for plump and playgrounds for
pasty children;
The police must be large, but little men are
hired to
Service the subterranean
Miles of dendritic drainage.

A married tribe commutes, mild from suburbia,
Whom ritual rules protect against raids by the
nomad
Misfortunes they fear; for they flinch in their
dreams at the scratch
Of coarse pecuniary claws, at crying images,
Petulant, thin, reproachful,
Destitute shades of dear ones.

Well, here I am but how, how, asks the visitor,
Strolling through the strange streets, can I start
to discover

The fashionable feminine fret, or the form of insult
Minded most by the men? In what myth do their sages
Locate the cause of evil?
How are these people punished?

How, above all, will they end? By any natural
Fascination of frost or flood, or from the artful
Obliterating bang whereby God's rebellious image
After thousands of thankless years spent in thinking about it,
Finally finds a solid
Proof of its independence?

Now a trolley car comes, going northward. They take it. Emble says:

This tortuous route through town
Was planned, it seems, to serve
Its institutions; for we halt
With a jerk at the Gothic gates
Of the Women's Prison, the whitewashed
Hexagonal Orphanage for
Doomed children, the driveway,
Bordered with trees in tubs
Of the Orthopædic Hospital,
And are crowded by the close relatives

Of suffering, who sit upright
With little offerings on their laps
Of candy, magazines, comics,
Avoiding each other's eyes,
Shy of a rival shame.

Slums are replaced by suburbs,
Suburbs by tennis-courts, tennis-courts
By greenhouses and vegetable gardens.
The penultimate stop is the State
Asylum, a large Palladian
Edifice in acres of grounds
Surrounded by iron railings;
And now there is no one left
For the final run through fields
But ourselves whose diseases as yet
Are undiagnosed, and the driver
Who is anxious to get home to his tea.

The buttercups glitter; our bell
Clangs loudly; and the lark's
Song is swallowed up in
The blazing blue: we are set
Down and do not care
Very much but wonder why.

Now they see before them, standing, half hidden by trees, on a little insurrection of red sandstone above a coiling river, the big house which marks the end of their journey's fourth stage. Rosetta is enthusiastic and runs forward saying:

In I shall go, out I shall look.

But the others are tired and Malin says:

Very well, we will wait, watch from outside.

QUANT says:

A scholarly old scoundrel,
Whose fortune was founded on the follies of others,
Built it for his young bride.
She died in childbed; he died on the gallows;
The property passed to the Crown.

The façade has a lifeless look,
For no one uses the enormous ballroom;
But in book-lined rooms at the back
Committees meet, and many strange
Decisions are secretly taken.

High up in the East Tower,
A pale-faced widow looks pensively down
At the terrace outside where the snow
Flutters and flurries round the formal heads
Of statues that stare at the park.

And the guards at the front gate
Change with the seasons; in cheerful Spring

How engaging their glances; but how
Morose in Fall: ruined kitchen-maids
Blubber behind the bushes.

Rosetta returns, more slowly than she left. Emble asks:

Well, how was it? What did you see?

ROSETTA answers: Opera glasses on the ormolu table
Frock-coated father framed on the wall
In a bath-chair facing a big bow-window,
With valley and village invitingly spread,
I got what is going on.

At the bend of the Bourne where the brambles grow thickest
Major Mott joins Millicent Rusk;
Discreetly the kingfisher keeps his distance
But an old cob swan looks on as they
Commit the sanguine sin.

Heavy the orchards; there's Alison pinching
Her baby brother, Bobby and Dick
Frying a frog with their father's reading-glass,
Conrad and Kay in the carpentry shed
Where they've no business to be.

Cold are the clays of Kibroth-Hattaavah,
Babel's urbanities buried in sand,

Red the geraniums in the rectory garden
Where the present incumbent reads Plato in
French
And has lost his belief in Hell.

From the gravel-pits in Groaning Hollow
To the monkey-puzzle on Murderer's Hill,
From the Wellington Arms to the white steam
laundry,
The significant note is nature's cry
Of long-divided love.

I have watched through a window a World that
is fallen,
The mating and malice of men and beasts,
The corporate greed of quiet vegetation,
And the homesick little obstinate sobs
Of things thrown into being.

I would gladly forget; let us go quickly.

EMBLE said: Yonder, look, is a yew avenue,
A mossy mile. For amusement's sake
Let us run a race till we reach the end.

This, willing or unwilling, they start to do and, as they run, their rival natures, by art comparing and compared, reveal themselves. Thus Malin mutters:

"Alas," say my legs, "if we lose it will be
A sign you have sinned."

And QUANT: The safest place
Is the more or less middling: the mean average
Is not noticed.

And EMBLE: How nice it feels
To be out ahead: I'm always lucky
But must remember how modest to look.

And ROSETTA: Let them call; I don't care. I shall keep them waiting.
They ought to have helped me. I can't hope to be first
So let me be last.

In this manner, sooner or later they come to the crumbling lichen-covered wall of the forgotten graveyard which marks the end of the fifth stage of their journey. At their feet lies a fallen wooden sign, bearing in faded letters the warning:

No Entrance Here Without a Subject

and underneath this, in smaller, barely decipherable script, some verses which Emble starts to read aloud:

Stranger, this still
Museum exhibits
The results of life:

Thoughtfully, therefore,
Peer as you pass
These cases clouded
By vetch and eyebright
And viper's bugloss
At each little collection
Loosely arranged
Of dated dust.

Here it is holy,
Here at last
In mute marble
The Master closed
His splendid period;
A spot haunted
By goat-faced grasshoppers
And gangling boys
Taunted by talents
Which tell them more
Than their flesh can feel.

Here impulse loses
Its impetus: thus
Far and no farther
Their legs, resolutions
And longings carried
The big, the ambitious,

The beautiful; all
Stopped in mid-stride
At this straggling border
Where wildflowers begin
And wealth ends.

Yet around their rest
Flittermice, finches
And flies restore
Their lost milieu;
An inconsequential
Host of pert
Occasional creatures,
Blindly, playfully,
Bridging death's
Eternal gap
With quotidian joy.

Malin sighs and says what they are all thinking but wish they were not.

Again we must digress, go by different
Paths in pairs to explore the land.

Knowing they will never be able to agree as to who shall accompany whom, they cast lots and so it falls out that Rosetta is to go with Quant and Emble with Malin. Two are disappointed, two are disturbed.

QUANT mutters: This bodes badly.

And MALIN: So be it. Who knows
If we wish what we will?

And ROSETTA: Will you forget
If you know that I won't?

And EMBLE: Will your need be me?

They depart now, Malin and Emble westward on bicycles, Quant and Rosetta eastward by boat, sad through fair scenes, thinking of another and talking to themselves.

MALIN says: As we cycle silent through a serious land
For hens and horses, my hunger for a live
Person to father impassions my sense
Of this boy's beauty in battle with time.

These old-world hamlets and haphazard lanes
Are perilous places; how plausible here
All arcadian cults of carnal perfection,
How intoxicating the platonic myth.

EMBLE says: Pleasant my companion but I pine for another.

QUANT says: Our canoe makes no noise; monotonous
Ramparts of reeds surround our navigation;

The waterway winds as it wants through the hush:

O fortunate fluid her fingers caress.

Welcome her, world; sedge-warblers, betray your
Hiding places with song; and eddy, butterflies,
In frivolous flights about that fair head:
How apt your homage to her innocent disdain.

ROSETTA says: The figure I prefer is far away.

MALIN says: To know nature is not enough for the ego;
The aim of its eros is to create a soul,
The start of its magic is stolen flesh.

QUANT says: Let nature unite us whose needs belong to
Separate systems that make no sense to each other:
She is not my sister and I am not her friend.

EMBLE says: Unequal our happiness: his is greater.

ROSETTA says: Lovelier would this look if my love were with me.

MALIN says: Girlishly glad that my glance is not chaste,
He wants me to want what he would refuse:
For sons have this desire for a slave also.

QUANT says: Both graves of the stream are agog as here
Comes a bride for a bridegroom in a boat ferried
By a dying man dreaming of a daughter-wife.

Now they arrive, two and two, east and west, at the hermetic gardens and the sixth stage of their journey is completed. They gaze about them entranced at the massive mildness of these survivals from an age of cypresses and cisterns.

ROSETTA says: How tempting to trespass in these Italian gardens
With their smirk ouches and sweet-smelling borders,
To lean on the low
Parapet of some pursive fountain
And drowse through the unctuous day.

EMBLE says: There are special perspectives for speculation,
Random rose-walks, and rustic bridges
Over neat canals;
A miniature railroad with mossy halts
Wambles through wanton groves.

QUANT says: Yet this is a theater where thought becomes act
And beside a sundial, in the silent umbrage
Of some dark daedal,
The ruined rebel is recreated
And chooses a chosen self.

From lawns and relievos the leisure makes
Its uncomfortable claim and, caught off its guard,
  His hardened heart
Consents to suffer, and the sudden instant
  Touches his time at last.

MALIN says: Tense on the parterre, he takes the hero's
Leap into love; then, unlatching the wicket
  Gate he goes:
The plains of his triumph appear empty,
  But now among their motionless

Avenues and urns with extra élan
Faster revolves the invisible corps
  Of pirouetting angels
And a chronic chorus of cascades and birds
  Cuts loose in a wild cabaletta.

Presently the extraordinary charm of these gardens begins to work upon them also. It seems an accusation. They become uneasy and unwell.

EMBLE says: I would stay to be saved but the stillness here
Reminds me too much of my mother's grief;
It scorns and scares me.

QUANT says: My excuses throb
Louder and lamer.

ROSETTA says: The long shadows
Disapprove of my person.

MALIN says: Reproached by the doves,
My groin groans.

ROSETTA: I've got a headache,
And my nose is inflamed.

QUANT: My knees are stiff.

EMBLE: My teeth need attention.

Then QUANT says: Who will trust me now,
Who with broad jokes have bored my children
And, warm by my wife, have wished her dead
Yet turned her over, who have told strangers
Of the cars and castles that accrued with the fortune
I might have made?

And EMBLE says: My mortal body
Has sinned on sofas; assigning to each
Points for pleasure, I have pencilled on envelopes
Lists of my loves.

And ROSETTA says: Alas for my sneers
At the poor and plain: I must pay for thinking
Failure funny.

And MALIN says: I have felt too good
At being better than the best of my colleagues:
Walking by water, have worked out smiling
Deadly reviews. My deeds forbid me
To linger longer. I'll leave my friend,
Be sorry by myself.

Then EMBLE again: I must slip off
To the woods to worry.

Then ROSETTA: I want to retire
To some private place and pray to be made
A good girl.

And then QUANT: I must go away
With my terrors until I have taught them to sing.

So one by one they plunge into the labyrinthine forest and vanish down solitary paths, with no guide but their sorrows, no companion but their own voices. Their ways cross and recross yet never once do they meet though now and then one catches somewhere not far off a brief snatch of another's song. Thus Quant's voice is heard singing:

A vagrant veteran I,
Discharged with grizzled chin,
Sans youth or use, sans uniform,
A tiger turned an ass.

Then MALIN'S: These branches deaf and dumb
Were woeful suitors once;
Mourning unmanned, and moping turned
Their sullen souls to wood.

Then ROSETTA'S: My dress is torn, my tears
Are running as I run
Through forests far from father's eye
To look for a true love.

Then EMBLE'S: My mother weeps for me
Who disappeared at play
From home and hope like all who chase
The blue elusive bird.

Now QUANT'S again: Through gloomy woods I go
Ex-demigod; the damp
Awakes my wound; I want my tea
But needed am of none.

Now EMBLE'S: More faint, more far away
The huntsman's social horn

Calls through the cold uncanny woods
And nearer draws the night.

Now ROSETTA'S:	Dear God, regard thy child; Repugn or pacify All furry forms and fangs that lurk Within this horrid shade.
Now MALIN'S:	Their given names forgot, Mere species of despair, On whims of wind their wills depend, On temperatures their mood.
And yet once more QUANT'S:	So, whistling as I walk Through brake and copse, I keep A lookout for the Limping One Who buys abandoned souls.

Obedient to their own mysterious laws of direction, their twisting paths converge, approach their several voices, and collect the four for a startled reunion at the forest's edge. They stare at what they see.

QUANT says:	The climate of enclosure, the cool forest Break off abruptly: Giddy with the glare and ungoverned heat, We stop astonished,

Interdicted by desert, its dryness edged
  By a scanty scrub
Of Joshua trees and giant cacti;
  Then, vacant of value,
Incoherent and infamous sands,
  Rainless regions
Swarming with serpents, ancestral wastes,
  Lands beyond love.

Now, with only the last half of the seventh stage to go to finish their journey, for the first time fear and doubt dismay them. Is triumph possible? If so, are they chosen? Is triumph worth it? If so, are they worthy?

MALIN says:

Boring and bare of shade,
Devoid of souvenirs and voices,
It takes will to cross this waste

Which is really empty: the mirage
Need not be tasty to tempt;
For the senses arouse themselves,

And an image of humpbacked girls
Or plates of roasted rats
Can make the mouth water.

With nothing to know about,
The mind reflects on its movements
And so doubles any distance.

Even if we had time
To read through all the wrinkled
Reports of explorers who claim

That hidden arrant streams
Chuckle through this chapped land
In profound and meagre fissures,

Or that this desert is dotted with
Oases where acrobats dwell
Who make unbelievable leaps,

We should never have proof they were not
Deceiving us. For the only certain
Truth is that they returned,

And that we cannot be deaf to the question:
"Do I love this world so well
That I have to know how it ends?"

EMBLE says:

As yet the young hero's
Brow is unkissed by battle,
But he knows how necessary
Is his defiance of fate
And, serene already, he sails
Down the gorge between the august
Faces carved in the cliffs
Towards the lordship of the world.

And the gentle majority are not
Afraid either, but, owl-like
And sedate in their glass globes
The wedded couples wave
At the bandits racing by
With affection, and the learned relax
On pinguid plains among
A swarm of flying flowers.

But otherwise is it with the play
Of the child whom chance decrees
To say what all men suffer:
For he wishes against his will
To be lost, and his fear leads him
To dales of driving rain
Where peasants with penthouse eyebrows
Sullenly guard the sluices.

And his steps follow the stream
Past rusting apparatus
To its gloomy beginning, the original
Chasm where brambles block
The entrance to the underworld;
There the silence blesses his sorrow,
And holy to his dread is that dark
Which will neither promise nor explain.

ROSETTA says: Are our dreams indicative? Does it exist,
That last landscape
Of gloom and glaciers and great storms
Where, cold into chasms, cataracts
Topple, and torrents
Through rocky ruptures rage for ever
In a winter twilight watched by ravens,
Birds on basalt,
And shadows of ships long-shattered lie,
Preserved disasters, in the solid ice
Of frowning fjords?
Does the Moon's message mean what it says:
"In that oldest and most hidden of all places
Number is unknown"?
Can lying lovers believe their bones'
Unshaken assurance
That all the elegance, all the promise
Of the world they wish is waiting there?

Even while she is still speaking, their fears are confirmed, their hopes denied. For the world from which their journey has been one long flight rises up before them now as if the whole time it had been hiding in ambush, only waiting for the worst moment to reappear to its fugitives in all the majesty of its perpetual fury.

QUANT says: My shoulders shiver. A shadow chills me
As thunderheads threaten the sun.

MALIN says: Righteous wrath is raising its hands
To strike and destroy.

EMBLE says: Storm invades
The Euclidean calm. The clouds explode.
The scene dissolves, is succeeded by
A grinning gap, a growth of nothing
Pervaded by vagueness.

ROSETTA says: Violent winds
Tear us apart. Terror scatters us
To the four coigns. Faintly our sounds
Echo each other, unrelated
Groans of grief at a great distance.

QUANT says: In the wild West they are whipping each other.

EMBLE says: In the hungry East they are eating their books.

ROSETTA says: In the numb North there are no more cradles.

MALIN says: The sullen South has been set on fire.

EMBLE says: Dull through the darkness, indifferent tongues
From bombed buildings, from blacked-out towns,

Camps and cockpits, from cold trenches,
Submarines and cells, recite in unison
A common creed, declaring their weak
Faith in confusion. The floods are rising;
Rain ruins on the routed fragments
Of all the armies; indistinct
Are friend and foe, one flux of bodies
Miles from mother, marriage, or any
Workable world.

QUANT says:

The wall is fallen
That Balbus built, and back they come
The Dark Ones to dwell in the statues,
Manias in marble, messengers from
The Nothing who nothings. Night descends;
Through thickening darkness thin uneases,
Ravenous unreals, perambulate
Our paths and pickles.

MALIN says:

The primary colors
Are all mixed up; the whole numbers
Have broken down, the big situations
Ceased to excite.

ROSETTA says:

Sick of time,
Long Ada and her Eleven Daughters,
The standing stones, stagger, disrupt

Their petrified polka on Pillicock Mound;
The chefs and shepherds have shot themselves,
The dowagers dropped in their Dutch gardens,
The battle-axe and the bosomed war-horse
Swept grand to their graves. Graven on all things,
Inscribed on skies, escarpments, trees,
Notepaper, neckties, napkin rings,
Brickwalls and barns, or branded into
The livid limbs of lambs and men,
Is the same symbol, the signature
Of reluctant allegiance to a lost cause.

MALIN says: Our ideas have got drunk and drop their H's.

EMBLE: We err what we are as if we were not.

ROSETTA: The honest and holy are hissed at the races.

QUANT: God's in his greenhouse, his geese in the world.

Saying this, they woke up and recognized where they sat and who they were. The darkness which had invaded their dream was explained, for it was closing time and the bartender was turning off the lights. What they had just dreamed they could no longer recall exactly, but when Emble and Rosetta looked at each other, they were conscious of some sweet shared secret which it might be dangerous to remember too well. Perhaps it was this which prompted Rosetta to suggest that they all come back to her apartment for a snack and a nightcap for, when they accepted, she realized that she had been expecting Quant and Malin to decline. But it was too late now. They were out in the street already and Emble had hailed a cab.

PART FOUR

THE DIRGE

His mighty work for the nation,
Strengthening peace and securing union,
Always at it since on the throne,
Has saved the country more than one billion

Broadsheet *on the death of King Edward VII*

As they drove through the half-lit almost empty streets, the effect of their dream had not yet worn off but persisted as a mutual mood of discouragement. Whether they thought of Nature, of her unending stream of irrelevant events without composition or center, her reckless waste of value, her alternate looks of idiotic inertia and insane ferocity, or whether they thought of Man, of the torpor of his spirit, the indigent dryness of his soul, his bottomless credulity, his perverse preference for the meretricious or the insipid—it seemed impossible to them that either could have survived so long had not some semi-divine stranger with superhuman powers, some Gilgamesh or Napoleon, some Solon or Sherlock Holmes, appeared from time to time to rescue both, for a brief bright instant, from their egregious destructive blunders. And for such a great one who, long or lately, has always died or disappeared, they now lamented thus.

Sob, heavy world,
Sob as you spin
Mantled in mist, remote from the happy:
The washerwomen have wailed all night,
The disconsolate clocks are crying together,
And the bells toll and toll
For tall Agrippa who touched the sky:
Shut is that shining eye
Which enlightened the lampless and lifted up
The flat and foundering, reformed the weeds
Into civil cereals and sobered the bulls;
Away the cylinder seal,
The didactic digit and dreaded voice
Which imposed peace on the pullulating
Primordial mess. Mourn for him now,
Our lost dad,
Our colossal father.

For seven cycles
For seven years
Past vice and virtue, surviving both,
Through pluvial periods, paroxysms
Of wind and wet, through whirlpools of heat,
And comas of deadly cold,
On an old white horse, an ugly nag,
In his faithful youth he followed
The black ball as it bowled downhill

On the spotted spirit's spiral journey,
Its purgative path to that point of rest
    Where longing leaves it, and saw
Shimmering in the shade the shrine of gold,
The magical marvel no man dare touch,
Between the towers the tree of life
    And the well of wishes
    The waters of joy.

    Then he harrowed hell,
    Healed the abyss
Of torpid instinct and trifling flux,
Laundered it, lighted it, made it lovable with
Cathedrals and theories; thanks to him
    Brisker smells abet us,
Cleaner clouds accost our vision
    And honest sounds our ears.
For he ignored the Nightmares and annexed
                                        their ranges,
Put the clawing Chimaeras in cold storage,
Berated the Riddle till it roared and fled,
    Won the Battle of Whispers,
Stopped the Stupids, stormed into
The Fumblers' Forts, confined the Sulky
To their drab ditches and drove the Crashing
    Bores to their bogs,
    Their beastly moor.

In the high heavens,
The ageless places,
The gods are wringing their great worn hands
For their watchman is away, their world-engine
Creaking and cracking. Conjured no more
By his master music to wed
Their truths to times, the Eternal Objects
Drift about in a daze:
O the lepers are loose in Lombard Street,
The rents are rising in the river basins,
The insects are angry. Who will dust
The cobwebbed kingdoms now?
For our lawgiver lies below his people,
Bigger bones of a better kind,
Unwarped by their weight, as white limestone
Under green grass,
The grass that fades.

But now the cab stopped at Rosetta's apartment house. As they went up in the elevator, they were silent but each was making a secret resolve to banish such gloomy reflections and become, or at least appear, carefree and cheerful.

PART V

THE MASQUE

"Oh, Heaven help me," she prayed, "to be decorative and to do right."

Ronald Firbank *The Flower beneath the Foot*

Rosetta had shown the men where everything was and, as they trotted between the kitchen and the living room, cutting sandwiches and fixing drinks, all felt that it was time something exciting happened and decided to do their best to see that it did. Had they been perfectly honest with themselves, they would have had to admit that they were tired and wanted to go home alone to bed. That they were not was in part due, of course, to vanity, the fear of getting too old to want fun or too ugly to get it, but also to unselfishness, the fear of spoiling the fun for others. Besides, only animals who are below civilization and the angels who are beyond it can be sincere. Human beings are, necessarily, actors who cannot become something before they have first pretended to be it; and they can be divided, not into the hypocritical and the sincere, but into the sane who know they are acting and the mad who do not. So it was now as Rosetta switched on the radio which said:

Music past midnight. For men in the armed
Forces on furlough and their feminine consorts,
For war-workers and women in labor,
For Bohemian artists and owls of the night,
We present a series of savage selections
By brutal bands from bestial tribes,
The Quaraquorams and the Quaromanlics,
The Arsocids and the Alonites,
The Ghuzz, the Guptas, the gloomy Krimchaks,
The Timurids and Torguts, with terrible cries
Will drag you off to their dream retreats
To dance with your deaths till the dykes
collapse.

Emble asked Rosetta to dance. The others sat watching. Quant waved his cigar in time to the music and sang a verse from an old prospector's ballad.

When Laura lay on her ledger side
And nicely threw her north cheek up,
How pleasing the plight of her promising grove
And how rich the random I reached with a rise.

Whereupon Malin sang a verse of a folksong from a Fen District.

When in wanhope I wandered away and alone,
How brag were the birds, how buxom the sky,

But sad were the sallows and slow were the brooks
And how dismal that day when I danced with my dear.

Moving well together to the music, Rosetta and Emble were becoming obviously attracted to each other. In times of war even the crudest kind of positive affection between persons seems extraordinarily beautiful, a noble symbol of the peace and forgiveness of which the whole world stands so desperately in need. So to dancers and spectators alike, this quite casual attraction seemed and was of immense importance.

Rosetta and Emble sang together:

Hushed is the lake of hawks
Bright with our excitement,
And all the sky of skulls
Glows with scarlet roses;
The melter of men and salt
Admires the drinker of iron:
Bold banners of meaning
Blaze o'er the host of days.

Malin has been building a little altar of sandwiches. Now he placed an olive upon it and invoked the Queen of love.

Hasten earthward, Heavenly Venus,
Mistress of motion, Mother of loves.

A signal from whom excites time to
Confused outbursts, filling spaces with
Lights and leaves. In pelagic meadows
The plankton open their parachutes;
The mountains are amused; mobs of birds
Shout at fat shopkeepers. "Shucks! We are free.
Imitate us—" and out of the blue
Come bright boys with bells on their ankles
To tease with roses Cartesian monks
Till their heads ache, geometers vexed by
Irrelevant reds. May your right hand,
Lightly alighting on their longing flesh,
Promise this pair what their prayers demand,
Bliss in both, born of each other, a
Double dearness; let their dreams descend
Into concrete conduct. Claim your own.

Rosetta and Emble had stopped dancing and sat down on the couch. Now he put his arm around her and said:

Enter my aim from all directions, O
Special spirit whose expressions are
My carnal care, my consolation:
Be many or one. Meet me by chance on
Credulous coasts where cults intersect
Or join as arranged by the Giants' Graves,
Titanic tombs which at twilight bring

Greetings from the great misguided dead;
Hide from, haunt me, on hills to be seen
Far away through the forelegs of mares;
Stay till I come in the startling light
When the tunnel turns to teach surprise,
Or face me and fight for a final stand
With a brave blade in your buffer states,
My visible verb, my very dear,
Till I die, darling.

Rosetta laid her head on his shoulder and said:

O the deep roots
Of the cross-roads yew, calm for so long,
Have felt you afar and faintly begin
To tingle now. What twitters there'll be in
The brook bushes at the bright sound of
Your bicycle bell. What barking then
As you stride the stiles to startle one
Great cry in the kitchen when you come home,
My doom, my darling.

They kissed. Then Emble said:

Till death divide
May the Four Faces Feeling can make
Assent to our sighs.

She said: The snap of the Three
Grim Spinning Sisters' Spectacle Case
Uphold our honors.

He said: The Heavenly Twins
Guard our togetherness from ghostly ills.

She said: The Outer Owner, that Oldest One whom
This world is with, be witness to our vows.

Which vows they now alternately swore.

If you blush, I'll build breakwaters.
When you're tired, I'll tidy your table.
If you cry, I'll climb crags.
When you're sick, I'll sit at your side.
If you frown, I'll fence fields.
When you're ashamed, I'll shine your shoes.
If you laugh, I'll liberate lands.
When you're depressed, I'll play you the piano.
If you sigh, I'll sack cities.
When you're unlucky, I'll launder your linen.
If you sing, I'll save souls.
When you're hurt, I'll hold your hand.
If you smile, I'll smelt silver.
When you're afraid, I'll fetch you food.
If you talk, I'll track down trolls.

When you're on edge, I'll empty your ash-tray.
If you whisper, I'll wage wars.
When you're cross, I'll clean your coat.
If you whistle, I'll water wastes.
When you're bored, I'll bathe your brows.

Again they embraced. Quant poured out the dregs of the glass on the carpet as a libation and invoked the local spirits.

Ye little larvae, lords of the household,
Potty, P-P, Peppermill, Lampshade,
Funnybone, Faucet, Face-in-the-wall,
Head-over-heels and Upsy-daisy
And Collywobbles and Cupboard-Love,
Be good, little gods, and guard these lives,
Innocent be all your indiscretions,
That no paranoic notion obsess
Nor dazing dump bedevil their minds
With faceless fears; no filter-passing
Virus invade; no invisible germ,
Transgressing rash or gadding tumor
Attach their tissues; nor, taking by
Spiteful surprise, conspiring objects
With slip or sharpness or sly fracture
Menace or mangle the morbid flesh
Of our king and queen.

Now, turning to Rosetta, Malin said:

O clear Princess,
Learn from your hero his love of play,
Cherish his childishness, choose in him
Your task and toy, your betrayer also
Who gives gladly but forgets as soon
What and why, for the world he is true to
Is his own creation; to act like father,
And beget like God a gayer echo,
An unserious self, is the sole thought
Of this bragging boy. Be to him always
The mother-moment which makes him dream
He is lord of time. Belong to his journey:
O rest on his rock in your red dress,
His youth and future.

Then, turning to Emble, he said:

And you, bright Prince,
Invent your steps, go variously about
Her pleasant places, disposed to joy;
O stiffly stand, a staid monadnock,
On her peneplain; placidly graze
On her outwash apron, her own steed;
Dance, a wild deer, in her dark thickets;
Run, a river, all relish through her vales.

Alcohol, lust, fatigue, and the longing to be good, had by now induced in them all a euphoric state in which it seemed as if it were only some trifling and easily rectifiable error, improper diet, inadequate schooling, or an outmoded moral code which was keeping mankind from the millennial Earthly Paradise. Just a little more effort, perhaps merely the discovery of the right terms in which to describe it, and surely absolute pleasure must immediately descend upon the astonished armies of this world and abolish for ever all their hate and suffering. So, such effort as at that moment they could, they made. Rosetta cried:

Let brazen bands abrupt their din and
Song grow civil, for the siege is raised.
The mad gym-mistress, made to resign,
Can pinch no more.

EMBLE cried: Deprived of their files,
The vice-squads cavort in the mountains,
The Visa-Division vouch for all.

Then ROSETTA: The shops which displayed shining weapons
And crime-stories carry delicate
Pastoral poems and porcelain groups.

Then EMBLE: Nor money, magic, nor martial law,
Hardness of heart nor hocus-pocus
Are needed now on the novel earth.

ROSETTA: Nor terrors, tides, contagion longer
Lustrate her stables: their strictures yield
To play and peace.

EMBLE: Where pampered opulent
Grudges governed, the Graces shall dance
In excellent order with hands linked.

ROSETTA: Where, cold and cruel, critical faces
Watched from windows, shall wanton putti
Loose floods of flowers.

EMBLE: Where frontier sentries
Stood so glumly on guard, young girls shall pass
Trespassing in extravagant clothes.

ROSETTA: Where plains winced as punishing engines
Raised woeful welts, tall windmills shall pat
The flexible air and fan good cows.

EMBLE: Where hunted hundreds helplessly drowned,
Rose-cheeked riders shall rein their horses
To smile at swans.

The others joined in chorus. Malin cried:

It is safe to endure:
Each flat defect has found its solid
Gift to shadow, each goal its unique
Longing to lure, relatedness its

Invariant base, since Venus has now
Agreed so gladly to guarantee
Plenty of water to the plants this year,
Aid to the beasts, to all human demands
Full satisfaction with fresh structures
For crucial regions.

QUANT cried: A kind word and
A fatherly peak not far away
For city orphans.

Then ROSETTA again: Synchronized watches
And a long lane with a lot of twists
For both sexes.

And EMBLE: Barns and shrubberies
For game-playing gangs.

QUANT: Grates full of logs and
Hinterland homes for old proconsuls
And pensioned pairs.

EMBLE: Places of silence
For real readers.

ROSETTA: A room with a view
For a shut-in soul.

MALIN: A shady walk
There and back for a thinker or two.

EMBLE: A gentle jaunt for dejected nerves
Over warm waters.

ROSETTA: A wild party
Every night for the outgoing classes.

MALIN: A long soliloquy to learn by heart
For the verbal type.

QUANT: Vast museums
For the acquisitive kind to keep tidy.

MALIN: Spigots to open for the spendthrift lot,
And choke-pear choices for champion wills.

Malin caught Quant's eye and they rose to take their leave. As they were getting their hats and coats, Quant sang:

O gifted ghosts, be gone now to affirm
Your dedication; dwell in your choice:
  Venus with grace preventing
  Requires what she may quicken.

Royal with roses be your resting place,
Balmy the airways, blue the welkin that

Attend your time of passage,
And easy seas assist you.

MALIN sang:

Redeem with a clear
Configuration
Of routes and goals
The ages of anguish,
All griefs endured
At the feet of appalling
Fortresses; may
Your present motions
Satisfy all
Their antecedents.

Rosetta went with them to the elevator. As they waited in the corridor for it to come up, Quant went on singing:

Wonder warm you with its wisdom now,
Genial joy rejuvenate your days,
A light of self-translation,
A blessed interior brightness,

Animate also your object world
Till its pure profiles appear again,
Losing their latter vagueness,
In the sharp shapes of childhood.

So did Malin as they entered the elevator:

Plumed and potent
Go forth, fulfill
A happy future
And occupy that
Permanent kingdom
Perameters rule,
Loved by infinite
Populations
Of possible cases:
Away. Farewell.

Then they sank from her sight. When she got back to her apartment, she found that Emble had gone into her bedroom and passed out. She looked down at him, half sadly, half relieved, and thought thus:

Blind on the bride-bed, the bridegroom snores,
Too aloof to love. Did you lose your nerve
And cloud your conscience because I wasn't
Your dish really? You danced so bravely
Till I wished I were. Will you remain
Such a pleasant prince? Probably not.
But you're handsome, aren't you? even now
A kingly corpse. I'll coffin you up till
You rule again. Rest for us both and
Dream, dear one. I'll be dressed when you wake
To get coffee. You'll be glad you didn't

While your headache lasts, and I won't shine
In the sobering sun. We're so apart
When our ways have crossed and our words
touched
On Babylon's banks. You'll build here, be
Satisfied soon, while I sit waiting
On my light luggage to leave if called
For some new exile, with enough clothes
But no merry maypole. Make your home
With some glowing girl; forget with her what
Happens also. If ever you see
A fuss forming in the far distance,
Lots of police, and a little group
In terrible trouble, don't try to help;
They'd make you mock and you might be
ashamed.
As long as you live may your lying be
Poetic only. I'd hate you to think
How gentile you feel when you join in
The rowdy cries at Rimmon's party;
"—Fasten your figleaf, the Fleet is in.
Caesar is sitting in solemn thought,
Do not disturb. I'm dying tonight with
The tragic poets—" for you'll trust them all,
Be at home in there where a host of creatures,
Shot or squashed, have insured good-luck to
Their bandit bodies, blond mausoleums

Of the inner life. How could I share their
Light elations who belong after
Such hopes end! So be off to the game, dear,
And meet your mischief. I'll mind the shop.
You'll never notice what's not for sale
To charming children. Don't choose to ask me.
You're too late to believe. Your lie is showing,
Your creed is creased. But have Christian luck.
Your Jesus has wept; you may joke now,
Be spick and span, spell out the bumptious
Morals on monuments, mind your poise
And take up your cues, attract Who's-Who,
Ignore What's-Not. Niceness is all and
The rest bores. I'm too rude a question.
You'd learn to loathe, your legs forget their
Store of proverbs, the staircase wit of
The sleep-walker. You'd slip and blame me
When you came to, and couldn't accept
Our anxious hope with no household god or
Harpist's Haven for hearty climbers.
So fluke through unflustered with full marks in
House-geography: let history be.
Time is our trade, to be tense our gift
Whose woe is our weight; for we are His Chosen,
His ragged remnant with our ripe flesh
And our hats on, sent out of the room
By their dying grandees and doleful slaves,

Kicked in corridors and cold-shouldered
At toll-bridges, teased upon the stage,
Snubbed at sea, to seep through boundaries,
Diffuse like firearms through frightened lands,
Transpose our plight like a poignant theme
Into twenty tongues, time-tormented
But His People still. We'll point for Him,
Be as obvious always if He won't show
To threaten their thinking in their way,
Nor His strong arm that stood no nonsense,
Fly, let's face it, to defend us now
When bruised or broiled our bodies are chucked
Like cracked crocks onto kitchen middens
In the time He takes. We'll trust. He'll slay
If His Wisdom will. He won't alter
Nor fake one fact. Though I fly to Wall Street
Or Publisher's Row, or pass out, or
Submerge in music, or marry well,
Marooned on riches, He'll be right there
With His Eye upon me. Should I hide away
My secret sins in consulting rooms,
My fears are before Him; He'll find all,
Ignore nothing. He'll never let me
Conceal from Him the semi-detached
Brick villa in Laburnum Crescent,
The poky parlor, the pink bows on
The landing-curtains, or the lawn-mower

That wouldn't work, for He won't pretend to
Forget how I began, nor grant belief
In the mythical scenes I make up
Of a home like theirs, the Innocent Place where
His Law can't look, the leaves are so thick.
I've made their magic but their Momma Earth
Is His stone still, and their stately groves,
Though I wished to worship, His wood to me.
More boys like this one may embrace me yet
I shan't find shelter, I shan't be at peace
Till I really take your restless hands,
My poor fat father. How appalling was
Your taste in ties. How you tried to have fun,
You so longed to be liked. You lied so,
Didn't you, dad? When the doll never came,
When mother was sick and the maid laughed.
—Yes, I heard you in the attic. At her grave you
Wept and wilted. Was that why you chose
So blatant a voice, such button eyes
To play house with you then? Did you ever love
Stepmother Stupid? You'd a strange look,
Sad as the sea, when she searched your clothes.
Don't be cruel and cry. I couldn't stay to
Be your baby. We both were asking
For a warmth there wasn't, and then wouldn't
write.
We mustn't, must we? Moses will scold if

We’re not all there for the next meeting
At some brackish well or broken arch,
Tired as we are. We must try to get on
Though mobs run amok and markets fall,
Though lights burn late at police stations,
Though passports expire and ports are watched,
Though thousands tumble. Must their blue glare
Outlast the lions? Who’ll be left to see it
Disconcerted? I’ll be dumb before
The barracks burn and boisterous Pharaoh
Grow ashamed and shy. *Sh‘ma‘ Yisra’el.*
a’donai ’elohenu, ’adonai ’echad.

PART VI

EPILOGUE

Some natural tears they drop'd, but wip'd them soon;
The world was all before them, where to choose . . .

John Milton *Paradise Lost*

Meanwhile in the street outside, Quant and Malin, after expressing their mutual pleasure at having met, after exchanging addresses and promising to look each other up some time, had parted and immediately forgotten each other's existence. Now Malin was travelling southward by subway while Quant was walking eastward, each to his own place. Dawn had begun to break.

Walking through the streets, Quant sang to himself an impromptu ballad:

> When the Victory Powers convened at Byzantium,
> The shiners declined to show their faces,
> And the ambiences of heaven uttered a plethora
> Of admonitory monsters which dismayed the illiterate.

Sitting in the train, Malin thought:

> Age softens the sense of defeat
> As well as the will to success,

Till the unchangeable losses of childhood,
The forbidden affections rebel
No more; so now in the mornings
I wake, neither warned nor refreshed,
From dreams without daring, a series
Of vaguely disquieting adventures
Which never end in horror,
Grief or forgiving embraces.

QUANT sang: But peace was promised by the public hepatoscopists
As the Ministers met to remodel the Commonwealth
In what was formerly the Museum of Fashion and Handicrafts,
While husky spectres haunted the corridors.

MALIN thought: Do we learn from the past? The police,
The dress-designers, etc.,
Who manage the mirrors, say—No.
A hundred centuries hence
The gross and aggressive will still
Be putting their trust in a patron
Saint or a family fortress,
The seedy be taking the same
Old treatments for tedium vitae,
Religion, Politics, Love.

QUANT sang: The Laurentian Landshield was ruthlessly gerrymandered,
And there was a terrible tussle over the Tethys Ocean;
Commentators broadcast by the courtesy of a shaving-cream
Blow by blow the whole debate on the Peninsulas.

MALIN thought:

Both professor and prophet depress,
For vision and longer view
Agree in predicting a day
Of convulsion and vast evil,
When the Cold Societies clash
Or the mosses are set in motion
To overrun the earth,
And the great brain which began
With lucid dialectics
Ends in a horrid madness.

QUANT sang: But there were some sensible settlements in the sub-committees:
The Duodecimal System was adopted unanimously,
The price of obsidian pegged for a decade,
Technicians sent north to get nitrogen from the ice-cap.

MALIN thought: Yet the noble despair of the poets
Is nothing of the sort; it is silly
To refuse the tasks of time
And, overlooking our lives,
Cry—"Miserable wicked me,
How interesting I am."
We would rather be ruined than changed,
We would rather die in our dread
Than climb the cross of the moment
And let our illusions die.

QUANT sang: Outside these decisions the cycle of Nature
Revolved as usual, and voluble sages
Preached from park-benches to passing fornicators
A Confucian faith in the Functional Society.

MALIN thought: We're quite in the dark: we do not
Know the connection between
The clock we are bound to obey
And the miracle we must not despair of;
We simply cannot conceive
With any feelings we have
How the raging lion is to lime
With the yearning unicorn;
Nor shall we, till total shipwreck
Deprive us of our persons.

Quant had now reached the house where he lived and, as he started to climb the steps of his stoop, he tripped and almost fell. At which he said:

> Why, Miss *ME*, what's the matter? *Must* you go woolgathering?
> Once I was your wonder. How short-winded you've gotten.
> Come, Tinklebell, trot. Let's pretend you're a thoroughbred.
> Over the hill now into Abraham's Bosom.

So saying, he opened his front door and disappeared. But Malin's journey was still not done. He was thinking:

> For the new locus is never
> Hidden inside the old one
> Where Reason could rout it out,
> Nor guarded by dragons in distant
> Mountains where Imagination
> Could explore it; the place of birth
> Is too obvious and near to notice,
> Some dull dogpatch a stone's throw
> Outside the walls, reserved
> For the eyes of faith to find.

Now the train came out onto the Manhattan Bridge. The sun had risen. The East River glittered. It would be a bright clear day for work and for war.

MALIN thought: For the others, like me, there is only the flash
Of negative knowledge, the night when, drunk, one
Staggers to the bathroom and stares in the glass
To meet one's madness, when what mother said seems
Such darling rubbish and the decent advice
Of the liberal weeklies as lost an art
As peasant pottery, for plainly it is not
To the Cross or to Clarté or to Common Sense
Our passions pray but to primitive totems
As absurd as they are savage; science or no science,
It is Bacchus or the Great Boyg or Baal-Peor,
Fortune's Ferris-wheel or the physical sound
Of our own names which they actually adore as their
Ground and goal. Yet the grossest of our dreams is
No worse than our worship which for the most part
Is so much galimatias to get out of
Knowing our neighbor, all the needs and conceits of
The poor muddled maddened mundane animal
Who is hostess to us all, for each contributes his
Personal panic, his predatory note
To her gregarious grunt as she gropes in the dark
For her lost lollypop. We belong to our kind,
Are judged as we judge, for all gestures of time
And all species of space respond in our own
Contradictory dialect, the double talk
Of ambiguous bodies, born like us to that

Natural neighborhood which denial itself
Like a friend confirms; they reflect our status,
Temporals pleading for eternal life with
The infinite impetus of anxious spirits,
Finite in fact yet refusing to be real,
Wanting our own way, unwilling to say Yes
To the Self-So which is the same at all times,
That Always-Opposite which is the whole subject
Of our not-knowing, yet from no necessity
Condescended to exist and to suffer death
And, scorned on a scaffold, ensconced in His life
The human household. In our anguish we struggle
To elude Him, to lie to Him, yet His love observes
His appalling promise; His predilection
As we wander and weep is with us to the end,
Minding our meanings, our least matter dear to Him,
His Good ingressant on our gross occasions
Envisages our advance, valuing for us
Though our bodies too blind or too bored to examine
What sorts excite them are slain interjecting
Their childish Ows and, in choosing how many
And how much they will love, our minds insist on
Their own disorder as their own punishment,
His Question disqualifies our quick senses,
His Truth makes our theories historical sins,
It is where we are wounded that is when He speaks

Our creaturely cry, concluding His children
In their mad unbelief to have mercy on them all
As they wait unawares for His World to come.

So thinking, he returned to duty, reclaimed by the actual world where time is real and in which, therefore, poetry can take no interest.

Facing another long day of servitude to wilful authority and blind accident, creation lay in pain and earnest, once more reprieved from self-destruction, its adoption, as usual, postponed.

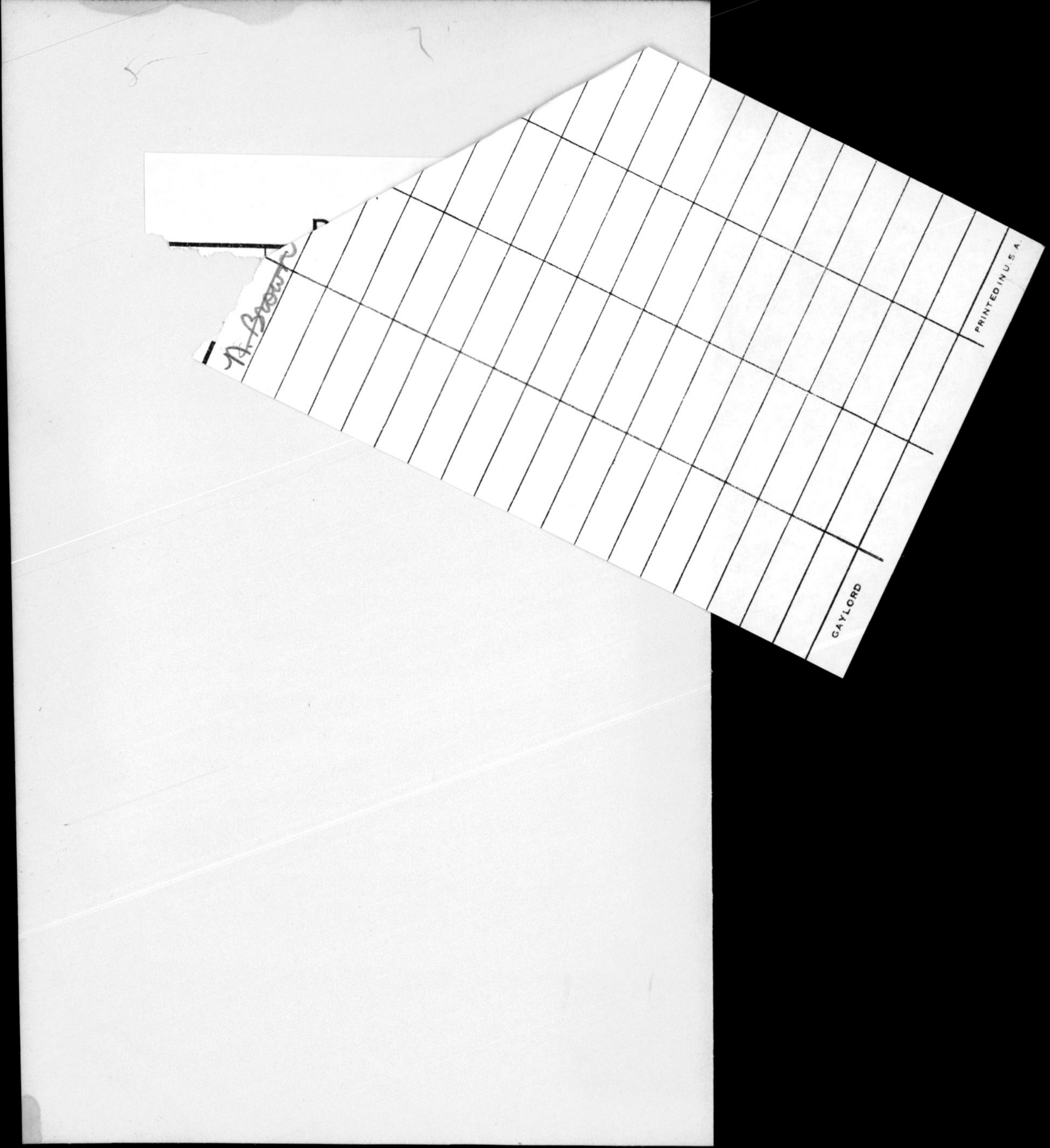
GAYLORD
PRINTED IN U.S.A.